Shells
of Britain and Europe

A CONCISE GUIDE IN COLOUR

Shells of Britain and Europe

by Jan Lellák

Illustrated by
Alena Čepická

Hamlyn
London · New York · Sydney · Toronto

Translated by Olga Kuthanová

Designed and produced by Artia for
The Hamlyn Publishing Group Limited
London – New York – Sydney – Toronto
Astronaut House, Feltham, Middlesex, England

ISBN 0 600 38020 3

Printed in Czechoslovakia

3/02/21/51

CONTENTS

FOREWORD

There are many people who do not live near the sea, who rarely have the opportunity of seeing the shells of molluscs. Certainly most are unaware of the range of types to be found.

For the person fortunate enough to live on the coast, or who often visits the seashore, the situation is quite different. Molluscs are to be found in almost every conceivable place – on rocks, in rock pools and in the sand at many different depths – often in huge numbers. This is not surprising when one considers that, in terms of numbers of species, molluscs comprise the second largest animal phylum in the world.

No-one can deny that some mollusc shells have an immediate beauty, whilst even those whose colours appear drab often have fascinating patterns of sculpturing. It is not surprising therefore that mollusc shells are collected the world over.

The sale of mollusc shells as souvenirs or ornaments can often form an important local industry. Apart from their ornamental value, many are of course also used as utility objects – ashtrays, dishes and cups for instance.

Perhaps the greatest pleasure comes from displaying shells as natural collections, for properly treated they can become beautiful objects of great durability.

Shells have fascinated mankind for centuries, and in history, their importance has been immense. Even to this day they form the basis of currency in certain parts of Asia and Africa. Certain species of mollusc yield the precious dye Tyrian purple. Garments dyed in this substance were a mark of the dignitary in ancient times.

Primitive tribes used shells as sacred vessels in religious

ceremonies, and before that, as water containers, roof tiles and wall decorations.

Part of the fascination of the study of shells – conchology – is to try and deduce the habits and life style of the shell's original owner. The vast variety of shell types is an indication of the diversity of molluscs.

The hardness and durability of mollusc shells have been useful features to man in yet another way. They are readily preserved as fossils that remain long after the animals inhabiting them have died. They therefore reveal much about the types of animal life that existed long ago, and their presence in certain rock types can give much information concerning the age of the rocks; i.e. they are index fossils.

The evolutionary history of molluscs can be traced back for hundreds of millions of years, and many species, extinct for millions of years, once occurred in vast numbers. Indeed, the living representatives of the phylum Mollusca as a whole are a mere fraction of the numbers that existed at the time of their greatest radiation, and point, sadly, to a declining group.

The molluscs chosen for this book are typical examples, common in the European seas. The aim of this book is to stimulate an interest not only in shells, but also in the animals that have built and inhabited them.

ABOUT MOLLUSCS IN GENERAL

Molluscs are a very ancient animal phylum which, during the course of evolution, have evolved into a vast number of forms. Today, there are some 112,000 known species of widely diverse shape and size, ranging from very small species hardly discernible with the naked eye to giants that are among the largest animals inhabiting the Earth. The Giant Squid (*Architeuthis dux*), for example, grows to as much as six and a half metres in length and its arms may be up to eighteen metres long!

Phylogenetically, molluscs split off from their marine worm-like ancestors a long time ago, forming a well-defined and independent animal phylum as far back as the Cambrian, the earliest geological period of the Paleozoic Era. At that time the phylum had already divided into several characteristic types based on morphological differences.

THE BODY STRUCTURE AND LIFE FUNCTIONS OF MOLLUSCS

The body of molluscs is usually bilaterally symmetrical (except in some gastropods) and is not divided into segments, nor does it have segmented limbs. It is usually soft, with no firm skeletal structure inside, and is almost entirely composed of connective tissue (mesenchyme) and muscles.

The body is divided into three more or less distinct parts: the head, the foot and the visceral mass.

In most species the anterior part of the body with the mouth opening and nerve centre forms a more or less distinct **head.** This may be surrounded by the anterior part of the foot. In cephalopods the head exhibits marked differentiation and structural modification. It is large and reinforced by an inner cartilaginous skeleton of its own and therefore cannot be pulled inside the foot. It is equipped with a mouth, generally located on the underside, sometimes one or more pairs of tentacles or arm-like appendages and also a pair of eyes. Bivalves lack a true head altogether.

The muscles are concentrated on the underside of the body and form a single large **foot.** The foot varies in shape and is usually the animal's only organ of locomotion. The highly developed ventral muscles have pushed the internal organs of molluscs to the dorsal part of the body. In the ancestral form the foot is a flat sole, covering nearly the whole of the underside of the body, which by contracting and relaxing the muscles and richly lubricating its path by secreting an abundance of mucus, enables the animal to crawl or glide forward. The concentration of body lymph in the foot enables it to expand into the shape of a firm club with which the animal may even burrow into the ground.

In some bivalves, glands located in a pit-like depression

on the underside of the foot secrete a mucus that rapidly hardens in the water to form a mass of tough threads called the byssus with which the mollusc can anchor itself firmly to rocks or other objects.

In freely swimming or freely floating molluscs the foot expands horizontally to form fins or wings. In the cephalopods the edges of the foot have developed into a ring of ten-

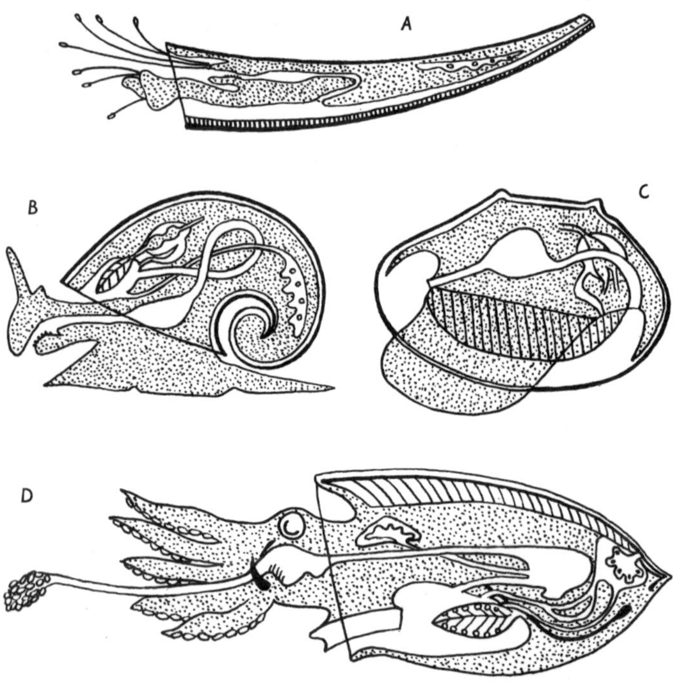

1. Diagram showing the body structure of the main types of molluscs:
A. Scaphopod B. Gastropod C. Bivalve D. Cephalopod.

tacles and a tube or funnel, serving as a special means of propulsion.

The **visceral mass** contains most of the internal organs. It is soft and the edges hang down in folds forming the **mantle** that covers the upper part of the foot. Between the mantle and body of the animal a space is formed called the **mantle cavity**; it contains the openings of the digestive, excretory and reproductive organs. Also suspended in this cavity are the respiratory organs or gills.

The body surface of molluscs has a great many mucus glands. The abundant secretion of mucus protects the body surface from damage and from drying out, at the same time lubricating it and thus greatly facilitating locomotion both in the water and on dry land.

The Protective Cover

In most molluscs the mantle secretes a protective cover in the form of a spiral, a tube, two saucer-shaped valves, or in some cases a number of lamellae. These covers have a complex structure and consist of several layers. The first is the outer surface layer, formed, as in worms, by chitinous organic matter called **conchiolin.** This layer covers the outside of the shell and is called the **periostracum.** In old, empty shells it may be wholly worn away.

The middle layer immediately beneath the periostracum is composed of calcium carbonate crystals arranged at right or oblique angles to the surface. This layer, called the **ostracum,** is of approximately equal thickness throughout and is secreted by the free edge of the mantle as the shell grows. It is this layer shining through that gives certain gastropod shells their glowing porcelain-like beauty. Its surface layer sometimes contains various bright pigments.

The inside of the shell adjoining the mantle and the visceral mass is formed by a third, inner layer called the **hypostracum.** This is secreted over the entire surface of the mantle and visceral mass in the form of thin sheets of aragonite laid down one over the other parallel to the surface on the inside wall of the shell, giving rise to the well-known mother-of-pearl layer. Its lustre and opalescent colours are caused by the refraction of light in the thin layers of the hypostracum. Nacre (mother-of-pearl) is continually secreted on the inside of the shell, adding to its thickness and weight.

In some groups of molluscs, evolution led to the gradual suppression of the growth and function of a heavy shell enclosing the body. True, such a shell shields the body from mechanical injury and from enemies, but at the same time has its unfavourable or negative aspects, mainly that it greatly limits the animal's freedom of movement. The gradual limitation of the shell's function began with the expansion of the mantle edge in certain molluscs and its curving back upward over the edge of the shell. As the supply of material for the growth of the shell gradually decreased, the shell became lighter and smaller until finally the mantle enveloped the whole shell. This further accelerated the degeneration of the shell, which in the end became merely a horny structure located under the skin on the top side of the body. This reduction of the shell may be found in certain terrestrial molluscs (slugs) as well as in some aquatic molluscs. One such example of a reduced shell is the familiar cuttlebone given by bird keepers to their pets.

The shells of molluscs are an inseparable part of the body and cannot be removed without serious damage to the inhabitants. Growth at the edge increases the size of the shell and the addition of new nacreous layers on the inside increases its thickness. These accretions to the shell make it possible to distinguish the periods of greater and lesser physiological activity, the latter being marked by a dark line, the former by a light line, much like the annual rings of trees.

As molluscs live in widely differing habitats, their shells are adapted to various modes of life. It is quite natural that the function and shape of a shell belonging to a mollusc that makes its home on the soft mud and sand of the seabed differ from those of species living on the hard rocky ground of the intertidal zone or of those that spend their entire lives near the surface of the open sea.

Internal Body Plan

It has already been stated that, in all probability, molluscs evolved from worm-like marine ancestors. This is also borne out by the internal plan of the body which over the ages underwent a number of changes. These were not only changes in shape but also changes in the location of certain internal organs when compared to the ancestral type, as well as the development of entirely new organs characteristic of the molluscs as a group.

At this point let us take a closer look at the molluscs' nervous system, the evolution of which has some very interesting aspects. In the more primitive forms, such as members of the group Amphineura, it is very simple and the nerve cells do not form well-defined ganglia. The nervous system consists of four nerve cords traversing the length of the body and joined together by numerous transverse cords.

In higher molluscs the nerve cells are clustered in paired (four to six) nerve masses (ganglia) joined together by filamentous bands. The individual pairs of ganglia are comparatively autonomous nerve centres, or local brains, that govern various parts of the body.

In most molluscs the conductivity of the nerves and their reaction, as well as the powers governing behaviour, are at a very low level. This elementary stage of development is markedly influenced by the limitation of most molluscs' food to plants or plant and animal debris. The formation of a strong and heavy protective cover and resulting limited mobility did not contribute to the development of these animals' nervous systems. An exception are the cephalopods, predatory creatures with the most highly developed nervous system in the entire phylum. They are very active animals, quickly reacting to stimuli. Also, the powers governing behaviour are on a far higher level than in other molluscs.

Widely varying degrees of development and perfection are exhibited by the light-receptive and visual organs of molluscs. In the most primitive forms the eyes are only flat depressions lined with light-receptive cells. The gradual deepening and closing of these depressions coupled with further differentiation led to the development of a very complex organ corresponding to the eye of vertebrates. The eyes of cephalopods have a lens, vitreous body and iris.

The mouth is generally equipped with a special file-like organ called the **radula.** It is a long, horny ribbon that moves forward and back over a cartilaginous base, a kind of rasp with which the animal can break up plant parts and scrape the algal covering off rocks and which also serves for boring into the shells, calcareous armour and skeletons of other molluscs, echinoderms and corals, as well as for the mastication of their fleshy parts.

Most molluscs have salivary glands that open into the buccal cavity. The saliva secreted by these glands serves primarily to facilitate the passage of food. In some molluscs, however, it contains acids that help disintegrate rocks and enable these creatures even to bore into hard limestone. In many predatory molluscs the saliva helps to soften and break up the calcareous shells of other molluscs.

Digestion in molluscs is carried out by a pair of large and greatly branched glands called the **hepatopancreas,** which secrete the chief digestive products into the stomach. In molluscs, however, we also find a primitive method of digestion characteristic of animals that are very low on the evolutionary scale. The food of mush-like consistency passes into the hepatopancreas, where particles are taken up by the individual cells of the inside walls and assimilated. In molluscs we thus find a combination of advanced extracellular and primitive intracellular digestion. The entire digestive tract, orginally more or less straight, is twisted to the side or forward, depending on the location of the mantle cavity in the body. The anus opens into the mantle cavity.

A further characteristic typical of all molluscs is the body space or pericardium. This is filled with fluid, and into it opens the ciliated funnel of the excretory organs (kidneys), which are generally paired. The copulatory organs originate by splitting off from the walls of the pericardium. Both the kidneys and copulatory organs open into the mantle cavity.

The remainder of the body space between the skin and digestive tract is filled with dense connective tissue (mesenchyme) interwoven with smooth muscles.

The circulatory system, which carries blood to all parts of the body, is very well developed in molluscs. Blood flow is regulated by the heart, located in the pericardium. The heart has as many auricles as there are gills in any given species of mollusc. In the ancient genus *Nautilus* the heart thus has four auricles. In other molluscs there are two, or more frequently only one, auricle opening into a single ventricle. In lower molluscs the circulation is not rigidly confined to a separate and independent system but mixes with lymph, the vital fluid thus being known as **haemolymph,** which is colourless. The respiratory pigment that ensures impregnation of blood with oxygen is **haemocyanin,** which imparts a blue colour to the blood.

The oxygenation capacity of the molluscs' blood is fairly low. Thus, for example, in the small squids of the genus *Loligo* the blood is capable of carrying about 4.2 percent of oxygen whereas in the terrestrial garden snail, only about 2 percent. For purposes of comparison, haemoglobin in human blood can carry 20 percent of oxygen.

The heartbeat of molluscs has a regular rhythm. Species that are comparatively inactive have about fifteen heart beats a minute at an ambient temperature of 20° C, more active species have sixty or more.

Closely associated with the circulatory system and its

main function, the supply of oxygen to various parts of the body, are the respiratory organs. As molluscs were originally marine animals, the original respiratory organs were gills or **ctenidia.** The gills of molluscs project into the mantle cavity. In various species they exhibit modifications that have occurred during the course of evolution. In the case of certain forms that have taken up life on dry land, these ctenidia have completely degenerated and have been replaced by a lung chamber, located in the mantle cavity.

The sexes in molluscs were originally separate but many species have become hermaphroditic, with a single individual producing both male and female cells. In the case of hermaphroditic molluscs the sex gland produces male cells first, the female cell, or egg, maturing later. During copulation hermaphrodites impregnate one another by exchanging sperm cells stored in a special part of the body until the eggs ripen and are fertilized. A special method of reproduction is found in the cephalopods in which the sexes are separate.

The eggs of molluscs are fairly large and are laid in batches, sometimes in gelatinous capsules or sheets of hardened mucus attached to various objects on the seabed. Terrestrial species lay their eggs in damp ground. Most marine molluscs hatch as ciliated larvae very like the larval trochophores of marine polychaete worms. The larvae of molluscs are, however, somewhat more developed on hatching and already have a shell which either continues to grow or disappears. They generally live as part of the plankton of the seas.

The anterior end of the larva has wing-like 'veils' fringed with fine hairs. The movement of these ciliated lobes, or **velum,** carries the larvae through the water thereby making them free-swimming. It is after this velum that this type of larva takes its name, being known as a **veliger.**

In cephalopods as well as other classes of molluscs, the egg contains a large yolk and embryonic development is of a higher degree; the veliger larva stage is absent and the young hatch as minute replicas of their parents.

THE EVOLUTION OF THE PHYLUM MOLLUSCA

It seems that the phylum Mollusca has already passed its zenith; this is borne out by the fact that molluscs had a far greater wealth of forms and species and were far more numerous, especially among the fauna of the sea, in past ages. Certain genera, families, and even orders, very widespread and divided into a great number of species and forms in the remote past, are today extinct.

The classification of each zoological group attempts to present a picture of the phylogeny or natural evolutionary relationships of the individual species and groups. In the phylum Mollusca there is a sequence from the lowest to the most highly organized forms. From the point of view of the phylum's evolution, however, the classes do not follow one another in direct succession. Detailed study of molluscs shows that here is a case of parallel evolution, which in many instances sprang from ancestors long extinct and quite unknown to us today.

The large phylum of Mollusca can be divided into two subphyla: Amphineura and Conchifera.

Amphineura are the most primitive of all existing molluscs. To this day they have retained certain anatomical features analogous to those of the annelids (worms). The mantle and shell have not developed into the form typical of the other groups of molluscs.

This subphylum, all its members being marine animals, embraces about 1,150 species divided into two classes. The members of the first class (Aplacophora), primitive worm-like creatures without a shell, are of little interest to collectors of remarkable and beautiful natural objects. On the other hand, certain members of the order Chitonidea belonging to the second class (Polyplacophora) may arouse the collector's interest.

Polyplacophora, or coat-of-mail shells, comprise more than a thousand species. The largest member, *Amicula stelleri* of the Pacific Ocean, reaches a length of up to thirty-three centimetres.

The body of coat-of-mail shells is usually a longish oval and is greatly flattened on the ventral side. The foot is a broad muscular plate that covers the entire underside of the body. The animal moves forward by successive contractions of the muscles in the form of transverse waves moving from the forward end to the rear.

The dorsal part of the body is covered by eight calcareous plates that overlap each other like the tiles of a roof. The plates are firmly attached to the body, but have a certain freedom of movement so that when alarmed, for instance, the animal can curl up into a ball by contracting the muscles on the underside of the body.

Unlike all other molluscs, coat-of-mail shells have numerous sensory cells located in the dorsal plates which grow through the shell to the surface. Some of these cells, especially in tropical species, join to form clusters thus giving rise to light-receptive organs resembling simple eyes.

The head is located just ahead of the front edge of the foot and covered from above by the edge of the mantle. On the underside of the head is the mouth and inside is a well-developed radula. The alimentary canal is terminated by the anus, located at the posterior end of the body.

The sexes are separate in coat-of-mail shells. The sex gland is usually simple but has two ducts, one on either side of the body, both opening into the gill chamber. Male glands are coloured red, female glands are greenish. Sometimes the female carries the fertilized eggs in the mantle groove to protect them, a rudimentary example of parental care.

The free-swimming, trochophore-type larvae hatch from the eggs. They have one eye on each side of the body behind the anterior ciliated lobe. During the larva's development the upperside becomes segmented and the ventral side grows a compact foot that covers its whole length. In time the surface segmentation of the upperside develops into eight dorsal plates which become calcareous. Thus the eight-segmented trochophore changes and develops into the coat-of-mail shell.

Coat-of-mail shells first appeared in the Silurian seas and have remained marine animals to this day. They occur mainly in the intertidal zone of the shore, where they live firmly attached to rocks and other solid objects. These creatures exhibit very little mobility. Some deep water species are carnivorous.

The second subphylum, and the one of greatest interest, is the Conchifera. Its members, as the Latin name indicates, generally bear a fully developed, typical shell and are divided into the following groups or classes: Gastropoda, Scaphopoda, Bivalvia and Cephalopoda.

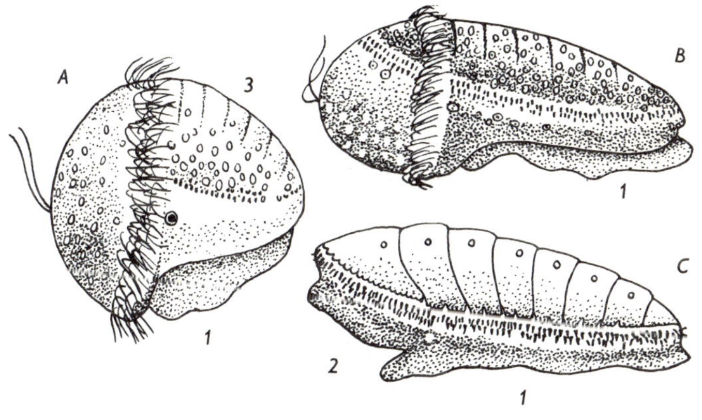

2. Stages of development of a chiton viewed from the side (A – C) 1. foot 2. head 3. basis of the shell.

GASTROPODA

This group of molluscs has the greatest number of species, some 85,000, showing marked diversity in size (the shell of the giant *Syrinx aruana* reaches a length of up to sixty centimetres). Embracing such a wide range of species, this group also exhibits a great diversity of shape and form. Gastropods are fairly active molluscs that have adapted themselves to a wide variety of food, thus being able to inhabit widely diverse habitats both in water and on dry land.

The external body structure of gastropods is very complicated. The whole of the underside forms a broad flat foot upon which the animal crawls or glides along by rhythmically contracting the longitudinal muscles. It furthermore secretes a continual flow of mucus for the lubrication of its path.

The adaptation of certain groups and species of gastropods to the specific conditions of a given environment has led to various changes in the shape of the foot. The most remarkable changes may be seen in the forms that abandoned the firm seabed to live and move about freely in the water. Here the foot has changed into a swimming organ of varying shape, generally simple vertical fins or paired wings.

The body proper consists of a large visceral hump which contains the internal organs. In most gastropods the body is distinctly separate from the foot and more or less twisted in a spiral. Hanging downward from the body is a fold of the mantle which forms the mantle cavity. In most gastropods the fold of the mantle and the mantle cavity is to be found in front, on the right-hand side of the body.

The Shell

The external cover, the shell, is secreted by the skin of the body. Shells show a marked diversity of shape and coloration. The basic type of gastropod shell, from which all others are derived, is a bilaterally symmetrical cone-shaped shell, e.g. that of the limpets of the genera *Patella* and *Diodora*. This type of tent-like shell covers the top and sides of the animal's body. Such a low cone with broad base is highly protective and makes it possible to live on rocks that are pounded by waves. These molluscs cling tightly to the rocks, which protect them from below, while the shell protects them from above and at the sides. A characteristic feature of most gastropod shells is that they coil in a spiral as they grow in length and breadth.

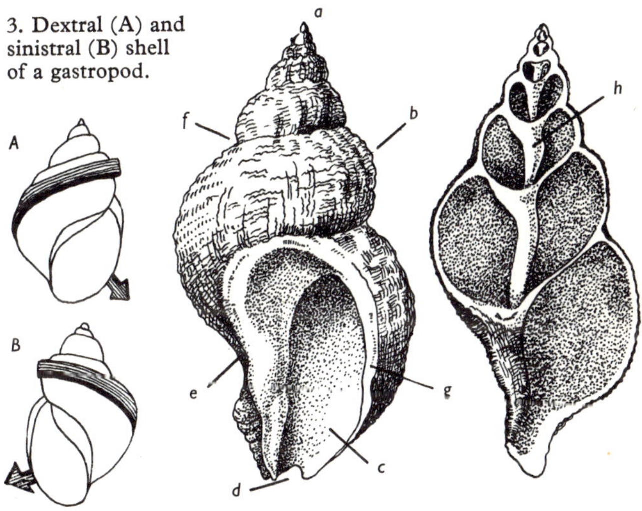

3. Dextral (A) and sinistral (B) shell of a gastropod.

4. Gastropod shell – overall view and cross-section: a) apex b) spire c) mouth d) siphonal canal e) umbilicus f) suture g) lip h) columella.

Basically, the gastropod shell is a tube which expands from the blind end at the top or apex towards the bottom, the widest part terminating in the mouth of the shell, the peristome, from which the animal extends its head and foot.

The spiral is generally conical and only in rare instances does it develop in a flattened form like a clock spring. Each new and larger coil is added to the preceding one. Shells in which the spiral twists to the right are called **dextral,** those in which it twists to the left are called **sinistral.** The former are the most common, the latter are more rare. Whether a shell is dextral or sinistral may be easily determined by holding it with the apex above and the aperture open toward the observer. If the aperture is at the right the shell is dextral, if it is at the left the shell is sinistral.

Other distinguishing features besides the apex, spiral and mouth include the suture, the line marking the junction of the whorls. The central axis is generally formed by a strong

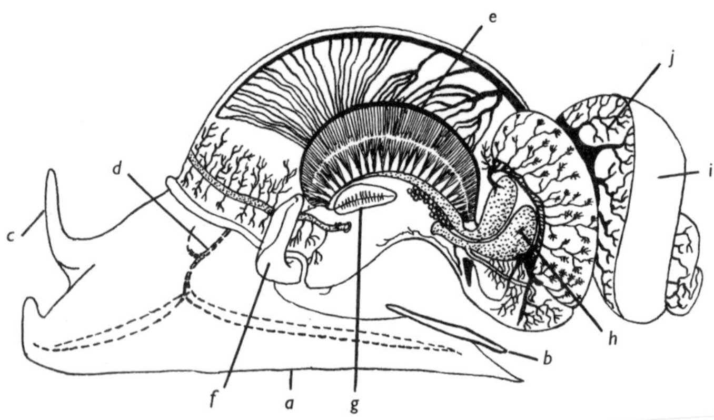

5. Body of a gastropod:
a) foot b) lid (operculum) c) tentacle d) pedal blood vessel
e) gill chamber blood vessel f) siphon g) osphradium
h) stomach i) gonad j) liver.

shaft called the columella, around which the shell is coiled. If the individual whorls are not immediately adjacent, i.e. do not touch on the inside, then no columella is formed and there is only a hollow shaft. Only in rare instances is the spiral loosely coiled and the whorls not in contact at all.

The shell of gastropods has no inside partitions. The visceral mass extends up to the apex, in other words to the earliest formed part of the shell. In a young animal the edge of the aperture or mouth is sharp and fragile. When the animal, and thus the shell, stops growing the edge of the mantle secretes a recurved lip (peristome). A thick lip indicates that the animal is an adult.

The molluscan shell is usually so spacious that the whole animal can conceal itself inside in case of need. In many prosobranchs (Prosobranchia) the foot is terminally capped with a horny or calcareous lid, the **operculum,** of about the same shape and size as the mouth opening. When the animal retreats inside its shell this lid fits tightly against the lip thus firmly closing the entrance.

In some species of marine gastropods the front edges of the mantle are joined together and drawn out into a tube of varying length called the siphon, which enables the animal to live embedded in sand or mud. Thus concealed the mollusc extends the siphon above the surface of the sand to suck water into the mantle cavity.

In some species of gastropods the shell is reduced or sometimes even completely absent. This may be found in both terrestrial as well as marine forms, in the latter case in benthic species that live on the sea bottom as well as in pelagic, or free-swimming, species.

Feeding and Digestion

The alimentary canal of the gastropods begins with the mouth, situated on the underside of the front end of the head. In some gastropods the mouth, instead of being a simple opening in the head, is located at the end of a blunt snout. In some predatory prosobranchs the whole front part of the head is extended to form a long trunk, or proboscis, which is retracted into the interior part of the alimentary canal and thrust out abruptly just before the animal grasps its prey. Behind the mouth cavity is the beginning of the gullet which contains the tongue or radula. It also contains jaws that are usually horny but are sometimes reinforced with calcium carbonate.

Opening into the gullet are two salivary glands. In some predatory gastropods, e.g. *Natica*, the acid saliva softens the calcareous shells or armour of their prey, usually other molluscs or echinoderms. Thus softened, the spot, about the size of the animal's proboscis, is easily bored with the radula and the proboscis is thereupon inserted through the opening to feed on the fleshy parts inside.

At the end of the long gullet is a sac-like stomach. Opening into the stomach is the liver (hepatopancreas), a large racemose organ. The liver plays the main role in the processing and assimilation of food.

From the stomach the food passes into the intestine and thence to the rectum. In lower prosobranchs of the order Diotocardia, the position of the digestive tract is very remarkable in that the rectum passes through the heart chamber.

Respiration and the Respiratory Organs

Gastropods originated in the sea and gills were the first form of respiratory apparatus for the exchange of gases. The first true gills were paired **ctenidia** located on either side of the anal opening. In some forms, however, we find partial reduction of the gills; the right ctenidium becoming smaller than the left, e.g. in ear-shells, until it completely degenerates. The change in the number of gill processes and in their location, e.g. under the heart (prosobranchs) or behind the heart (opisthobranchs) is an indication of evolutionary changes and also of the gastropods' adaptation to the changing conditions of their environment. The place of the aborted ctenidia was usually taken by other respiratory organs. In gastropods that live in water various substitute processes may be found on all parts of the body though these are not of the same origin as gills. They may be in the form of numerous finger-like projections on the edge of the mantle, e.g. in the limpet *Patella*, or sometimes in the form of a ring of plume-like outgrowths around the anal opening, etc. All these outgrowths, however, have one single task – to take over and replace the physiological function of the gills. In many gastropods living in water the reduction of the respiratory apparatus goes even further. They possess no special breathing organs at all but absorb oxygen through their skin.

In forms that took to living on dry land the gills are altogether absent. Here the blood capillaries, so abundantly distributed throughout the gills of species living in water, form a dense network of branching vessels immediately beneath the fine skin of the mantle cavity. The mantle cavity thus becomes a lung chamber whose inner wall absorbs oxygen and releases carbon dioxide. Some gastropod molluscs of the order Pulmonata, however, later returned from life on land to life in freshwater. Though they became aquatic animals again in a relatively short time, the aborted organs could not be rapidly replaced and so these molluscs must come to the surface regularly to recharge their lung chambers with air.

The Heart and the Circulatory System

In the most primitive groups of gastropods the heart has two auricles and one ventricle (two auricles because these molluscs still have paired gills). The gradual reduction of one gill is accompanied by a change in the shape of the heart and the gradual disappearance of the right auricle, the heart then consisting of one auricle (the original left) and one ventricle.

Arterial blood, i.e. blood that has been oxygenated in the gills or lungs, flows into the one or two auricles and thence into the ventricle from which it passes into the aorta that shortly divides into two branch arteries. The anterior artery supplies blood to the head and foot, and the posterior or visceral artery supplies blood to the intestines, liver and sex glands. From further branching vessels the blood is carried into minute lacunae (lacunae are body spaces that surround the internal organs), is deoxygenated, and gradually collects in larger venal lacunae. From there the blood flows through veins to the respiratory apparatus (gills or lungs), where it receives oxygen, and then flows back again into the heart.

The blood of gastropod molluscs is usually colourless and contains leucocytes resembling amoebas. Sometimes dissolved in this vital fluid is a proteinaceous substance similar to haemoglobin that functions as a respiratory pigment in a similar manner to haemoglobin in vertebrates. The blood of some gastropods was found to contain manganese, which apparently has a similar function to that of iron in the blood of higher animals, i.e. binding oxygen and transferring it to the body organs.

Besides the basic functions, i.e. supplying nourishment and oxygen and carrying off waste products, the blood of gastropods has a further important mechanical role. It serves to swell certain parts of the body, which is made possible by regulating the amount of blood in the many lacunae contained therein, thus allowing the animal to emerge from its shell, expand and harden its foot when it moves, and so on. Here we have the reason for the great amount of blood contained in the body of molluscs, sometimes as much as fifty percent of the body weight.

The Kidneys and the Excretion of Waste Products

The more primitive gastropods still have two kidneys, of which the left is generally smaller. In most forms, however, there has been a reduction of this organ, just as in the case of the respiratory organs or gills, and the animal possesses only the left kidney. This begins with a broad funnel in the pericardium and opens into the mantle cavity, usually immediately next to the anal opening.

The Nervous System

We have already seen in the lower prosobranchs the beginning of a concentration of the nerve cells into groups. This concentration of nerve cells gradually led to the development of a nervous system consisting of a number of knots or ganglia connected only by nerve threads without nerve cells.

The ancestral type of this system may still be found in the primitive ear-shells, *Haliotis*. Here the 'brain' forms a ring around the gullet from which two pedal nerve threads connected by small loops (commissures) extend along the ventral side. The simplest form of nervous system consists of five pairs of knots or ganglia which autonomously innervate most parts of the body, i.e. the foot and its muscles, the mantle and mantle cavity, the visceral mass and organs contained therein, as well as the mouth organs and gullet.

All pairs of ganglia are directly or indirectly connected by nerve threads to the cerebral ganglia, the chief governing centres also innervating the entire head, eyes, tentacles, organs of equilibrium, tactile organs and organs of smell.

Evolutionary development brought marked changes in the basic plan of the nervous system of gastropods, culminating in body asymmetry in higher forms. This change in body symmetry led to the crossing of nerve connections and the corresponding shift of the left ganglion to the right side and vice versa.

The Senses

Located in the skin and scattered over the whole body surface are numerous individual sensory cells which apparently react to mechanical and chemical stimuli. Large numbers are to be found especially on the tentacles, on the edge of the foot and on the fringes of the mantle.

Practically all gastropod molluscs have a pair of eyes carried on the head at the base or top of the second pair of tentacles. These range from simple depressions in the epidermis to very complex eyes with a lens and vitreous body.

The organs of equilibrium in all gastropods are a pair of **statocysts** located in the foot. These are fluid-filled vesicles in which are suspended a number of particles of calcium carbonate called statoliths. Their location and thus the pressure exerted on various sensory cells permits the animal to orientate itself in space and maintain its normal position.

Reproduction and the Copulatory Organs

Members of the most primitive gastropods of the order Prosobranchia are almost all unisexual. The more highly organized opisthobranchs and pulmonates are all hermaphroditic. All gastropod molluscs have one single sex gland which in the unisexual forms functions either as an ovary or testis. In the hermaphroditic forms it is called an ovo-testis and produces both egg and sperm cells.

The entire reproductive apparatus is extremely complex and includes a number of supplementary organs and glands, of which those that produce mucus aid in copulation and serve to encase the eggs in protective gelatinous covers. In hermaphroditic individuals fertilization is mutual, with both exchanging sperm cells during copulation so that each simultaneously functions as both male and female.

Development from the Egg to the Adult

The comparatively small and inactive gastropods usually lay their eggs in gelatinous masses that are either soft or hardened into the consistency of parchment. These are attached either to solid objects such as rocks, clumps of coral and sponges, sea grass and seaweed or to the sea bottom; or else they float freely in the water. The development of the embryo in the egg is very complicated and the ciliated larva that hatches usually shows not the least resemblance to the parent.

The veliger larvae of gastropods, however, differ from similar larvae of other molluscs in certain properties. After a time the skin on the upperside of the body forms a fold and in the resulting depression the gland is formed which secretes a thin horny plate, the basis of the future shell. Other parts of the larva's body develop into the foot, tentacles and eyes, and also the mantle of the future animal. Occurring simultaneously are complex changes in the internal structure.

Towards the end of this metamorphosis the free-swimming larva loses its chief organ of locomotion, the ring of moving cilia, and settles on the seabed. From this moment the animal switches to the benthic way of life, i.e. on the sea floor on various solid objects. This larval stage occurs in all marine prosobranchs and opisthobranchs. The eggs of freshwater snails and pulmonates have a greater quantity of nutritive yolk so that there is no larval stage and the young hatch as small replicas of the adults, equipped for life in the water.

Mode of Life

Gastropods were originally inhabitants of the sea floor. All members of the order Opisthobranchia and most members of the order Prosobranchia still inhabit this environment today. In the latter group, however, we find the first pioneers to venture forth into new territory, who adapted themselves to life in freshwater. Included among them are the widely distributed members of the genera *Viviparus* and *Bithynia*, which may be found on the bottom of stony banks and among the vegetation growing in various reservoirs and in large rivers.

Far greater strides in adaptation to life on dry land were made by the pulmonates (order Pulmonata), which were made possible by a radical change in their respiratory apparatus. Instead of gills, which absorb oxygen from water, they developed organs resembling lungs which enabled them to receive oxygen from the atmosphere. Most of these gastropods were thus able to abandon life in the water and adapt themselves to a permanent life on dry land. (Here we should point out, however, that a great many terrestrial species have returned to live in freshwater though they continue to take oxygen from the air.) Their remarkable ability to adjust to widely varied, often extremely unfavourable living conditions, enabled the pulmonate gastropods to survive in their new environment. They inhabit not only damp areas but some can also tolerate long periods of water shortage. They have settled in very dry places, some species even occurring in large numbers in steppe and desert regions. Others are tolerant of very low temperatures and may be found in polar and subpolar regions.

Pulmonates are able to survive great changes in temperature because they can induce a winter sleep during temporary spells of very cold weather and, vice versa, survive the heat of high summer by falling into a summer sleep. The animal does not feed, the heartbeat slows down, and the exchange of gases and other physiological functions are reduced to the minimum. The ability of these molluscs to sleep for long periods of time increases their life span sometimes to incredible lengths. There have been recorded instances where some individuals came to life after being museum exhibits for a number of years.

At first glance gastropods seem to be quite helpless creatures. This is far from true of the group as a whole, however, for these slow-moving animals have a number of ways of protecting themselves effectively. The simplest means of protection is the shell, into which the animal can retreat fairly rapidly. The shell's protection may be increased by having the aperture strongly narrowed and, often, toothed. A higher degree of passive protection is found in the prosobranchs, most of which are provided with an operculum on the foot that firmly closes the aperture like a lid when the animal retreats into its shell. The abundant secretion of slime or mucus also serves to protect the animal, for instance against small predators which are thus unable to get a foothold. Certain more active species, especially pelagic marine gastropods, can save themselves from slower-moving enemies by taking advantage of their ability to make a rapid escape. Crawling species that make their home on the seabed are usually too slow to escape by such means but make use of other ingenious methods. Members of the genus *Nassa* and *Cardium*, for instance, turn a kind of somersault to get away when danger threatens. Other species burrow rapidly into the seabed or conceal themselves among clumps of vegetation.

Molluscs, however, also include a number of forms that even put up an active defence which may prove very effective not only against an enemy but also against the curious and careless observer or collector. An example of such a method of active defence is provided by the Knobbed Triton *(Tritonium nodiferum)* which chases an enemy away or renders it harmless with heavy blows of its shell. To come across larger members of the genus *Strombus* may prove very unpleasant even for man as when these gastropods are threatened by danger they defend themselves by rapidly snapping the posterior end of the foot from side to side. As this part of the foot is covered with a hard lid or operculum that has very sharp edges, it may inflict deep wounds. Severe, sometimes even mortal, wounds may be inflicted by members of the genus *Conus*, which possess a poison gland that injects its venom into wounds made by a special dart in the proboscis.

SCAPHOPODA

Scaphopods, or tusk shells, include only a very small number of marine molluscs that combine the characters of both gastropods (univalves) and bivalves. A distinguishing feature of these molluscs is a long, almost cylindrical body encased in a slender tubular shell that is open at each end. The shell looks very much like a miniature elephant tusk, not only in shape but also in coloration, and this has given these molluscs the name by which they are known in all languages.

No less remarkable is the greatly simplified organization of the body. Tusk shells do not possess a well-defined head, this part of the body consisting of only a lobe with a funnel-shaped mouth. On either side of the mouth are bunches of long filaments with club-shaped tips serving as tactile organs and for catching prey. On the underside, below the head lobe, is a cylindrical, trilobed foot superbly adapted for ploughing through the seabed. Its terminal part is bluntly conical and used for digging into sand while the two side lobes serve as anchorage. Expanding with the inflow of blood, the foot is exserted from the shell and is retracted with the aid of muscles. By successive expansion and retraction of the foot the tusk shell moves forward along the seabed.

The internal organization of the body is very similar to that of gastropods. Tusk shells have jaws and a radula, similarly formed, an alimentary canal with a paired liver and a similar nervous system. They have no gills or lungs, however, and absorb oxygen through the surface of the mantle.

Tusk shells are very active animals that are almost constantly on the move and therefore possess very good organs of equilibrium with numerous statoliths and very sensitive tactile organs. Though they have no eyes they can perceive light and are photophobic (i.e. shun light). If light falls suddenly on their body, they rapidly retreat into their shell. The shape of both body and shell, the unusual body organization and the intolerance of light are all adaptations to an unusual way of life. These animals live constantly on the sandy sea bottom in which they burrow. They live almost entirely embedded in the sand with only one to two millimetres of the posterior end protruding above the surface. These small molluscs do not burrow vertically, but at a forty-five degree angle, which makes the process much easier.

Tusk shells have very mobile tentacles and also glands producing a sticky fluid which enable them to capture minute foraminiferans which form their diet. These are carried to the mouth by the filaments. From time to time the tusk shells move to a new feeding area, thereupon resuming their thorough search of the surroundings with the tentacles. They are most active at night.

The sexes are separate in this group of molluscs. The eggs, fertilized in the water, hatch into trochophore-type larvae that live among the plankton of the sea. In the larval stage the animal has a small saucer-like shell which changes its shape as the mantle grows. The mantle first grows on the dorsal side of the larva in the form of a paired fold. Only later does it become united on the ventral side to form a tube.

The tusk shells include only four genera with a greater number of species. They inhabit all types of sandy and muddy bottoms from the shoreline to great depths. Some are often found at depths of as much as 4,000 metres. They are distributed throughout most of the world but are partial to the warm seas of the tropics. In colder oceans the coloration of the shells is very simple, usually only white. In tropical seas, however, the shells are very brightly coloured, generally pink, lemon-yellow or the colours of the rainbow.

Tusk shells are of comparatively little practical use to man, being employed mostly by natives in certain tropical regions to make ornamental objects.

BIVALVIA

Bivalves seem to have very little in common with other molluscs at first glance, but the internal organization of the body indicates that they all belong to this large phylum.

There are about 25,000 known species of molluscs in the world. In such an abundance of species there are naturally great differences in size, ranging from several millimetres in length to veritable giants. The largest shell, beloging to the species *Tridacna gigas* which makes its home in the Indian Ocean, measures up to one and a half metres in length and weighs more than 250 kilograms. No doubt it takes its Latin name from the legendary giants of Homer's tales.

The body structure of all bivalves has a number of characteristic features. Apart from a few rare exceptions it is bilaterally symmetrical and greatly flattened on the sides. Bivalves do not possess a true head. The body consists of only a trunk and a foot. Located at the anterior end of the trunk is the mouth and at the posterior end, at about the same level, is the anal opening. Between these regions is the strong, muscular foot, located on the ventral side of the body.

In some very primitive species the foot has a flat sole, as in gastropods. In most bivalves, however, it is greatly flattened at the sides and shaped like a hatchet. Such a foot is not particularly useful for locomotion on firm ground, but is excellent for creeping along as well as for burrowing through soft, loose matter. This is fully utilized by the bivalves, many of them finding permanent shelter and protection from enemies in the mud and sand of the sea bottom. Cockles *(Cardium)*, which have a turgid curved foot, move with considerable speed in a series of jumps, covering up to several centimetres by extending the foot and then violently contracting the muscles. In some sedentary species living permanently in one spot, the foot has dwindled to small proportions (mussel, *Mytilus*) or has disappeared altogether (oyster, *Ostrea*).

In many bivalves the skin glands, massed in a depression on the underside of the foot, secrete a sticky matter that hardens rapidly in water into a mass of tough threads called the byssus. These elastic, silk-like fibres serve to anchor the mollusc to the bottom or to various solid objects in the water. Some molluscs are able to climb the smooth steep walls of underwater cliffs with the aid of these byssal threads and in a like manner the smooth slippery walls of an aquarium. True masters of this art are the edible mussels. In certain large species of bivalves, such as *Pinna*, these fine, firm threads are very long, and since ancient times have been spun and woven into fine fabrics as is done with the threads of the silkworm. There is no reason to doubt that the precious and costly fabric bysson, mentioned in the Bible, was woven from the byssal threads of bivalves, which has continued to be made into fancy goods even in the age of wool, cotton and man-made fibres. In the Mediterranean, byssal threads are employed in making exclusive gloves, belts and other clothing accessories.

A further characteristic organ of bivalves is the mantle, which greatly overhangs the body and forms a large sheet

6. How a cockle makes its escape when attacked by a starfish.

of tissue underneath the valves. The mantle edge bears three folds. Between these folds and the body is the mantle cavity which contains the gills and the foot. The mantle of bivalves fully deserves this name for it truly enfolds the body like a cloak, the two halves fitting tightly together when the shells are closed. In some species the margins are even united. No cloak can have its edges joined completely, however, for it must allow its wearer some freedom of movement as well as communication with the external environment. This is also the case in bivalves, where the mantle is only partially closed. The edges of the folds are usually joined only at two points so that there are three openings instead of a single slit. Through the large opening on the ventral side the animal extends its foot. At the posterior end of the mantle there are two elliptic openings, the lower one fringed with rows of sensitive tentacles, the upper one entirely smooth. It is through the lower opening that water flows into the mantle cavity, bringing the oxygen needed for breathing. It also brings with it minute food particles, which the animal filters out of the water. Here we have the explanation for the sensitive tentacles round the opening – they serve as 'sentries', intended to prevent the penetration of an unwanted guest, such as a parasite, into the mantle cavity. When these ten-

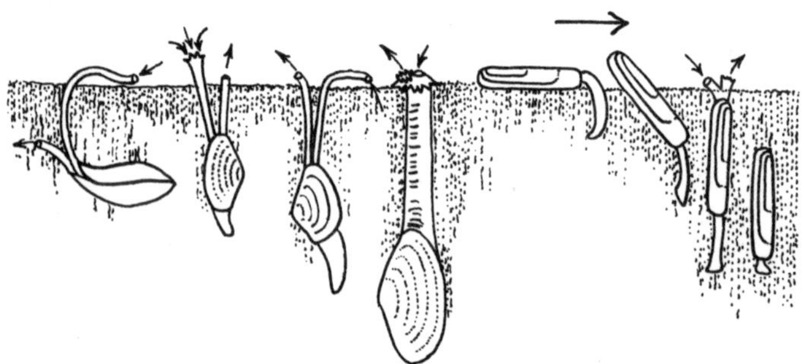

7. How some bivalves burrow in the mud and sand of the sea floor.

tacles are irritated the opening immediately closes, just like the portcullis in a fortress The water leaves the mantle cavity through the smooth upper opening, which also serves for the discharge of waste products carried out with the water. The edges of the incurrent and excurrent openings are often extended into muscular tubes called the siphons. Sometimes the siphons are joined together, sometimes they may be partly or entirely separate. Elongated siphons are characteristic of molluscs that burrow in soft sand and therefore the species that live buried deep in the sand and mud possess exceptionally long ones. The siphons are extended above the seabed surface, thus ensuring a regular supply of freshwater and food without the animals having to abandon their safe hiding place.

The siphons always project from the shells at the posterior end and the muscular foot is extended from the anterior end.

The Shell

As in most molluscs, the substance that forms the shell of bivalves is secreted by the outside of the mantle next to the shell and the shell is a faithful replica of the mantle. Even though it exhibits various adaptations to the conditions of life of the given species it is always a paired shell consisting of two halves or valves, by which bivalves differ markedly from scaphopods, which possess a one-piece shell.

In most species of bivalves the two halves of the shell are equal in both size and shape and enclose the body from both sides. Less common are shells with each valve different, this being mainly in the bivalves that live permanently in one spot, firmly attached to the substratum. In such a case the valve that is cemented fast forms a sort of cup or bed for the animal, is larger and more concave than the other valve and covers the whole body. The upper valve does not have to be as strong, is usually smaller and forms a lid to the cup. The most familiar example of such an asymmetrical shell is that of the oyster. In some bivalves, however, the shell is greatly reduced in size, for example in the Ship Worm *(Teredo navalis)*, where it has lost its protective function due to the animal's way of life and is reduced to two tiny valves covering only about one-twentieth of the body.

Because the bivalve shell is not only strong but often very heavy, it must be firmly attached to the body of the animal. It is usually firmly attached to the mantle at least near the edge of the shell on the outer margin of the folds of the mantle.

Upon opening the shell of a bivalve, for instance a species of cockle *(Cardium)*, it can be seen that the two shell halves interlock precisely at the apex. This part of the shell is equipped with a very ingenious system called the cardo, which consists of a row of knobs and teeth on one valve and corresponding depressions on the other valve, so that the two parts interlock. This system of lock and key is so specific for each species of bivalve that the left and right halves of the shell close perfectly only if they are the two halves of one

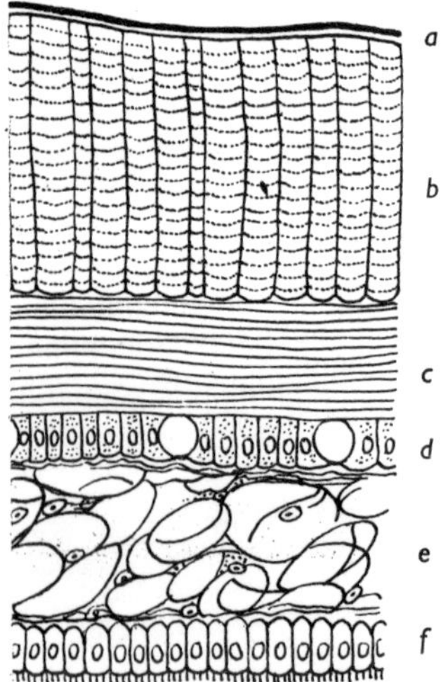

8. Cross-section of the shell and mantle of a bivalve:
a) outermost chitinous layer (periostracum)
b) porcellaneous crystalline layer (ostracum)
c) mother-of-pearl layer
d) outer lining of the mantle
e) connective tissue
f) inner lining of the mantle.

9. Bivalves boring in hard substances:
a) *Lithophaga*
b) *Gastrochaena*
c) *Pholas*
(The arrows indicate the path of the water current bringing oxygen to the gills.)

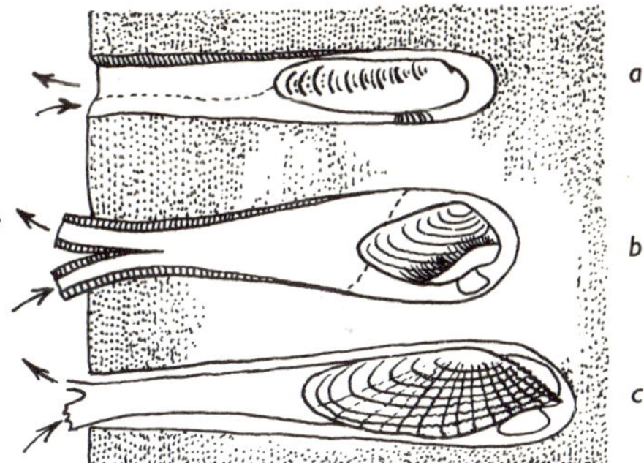

and the same individual or at most of two equal-sized individuals of the same species.

This system is supplemented by a further ingenious apparatus that serves to open and close the shell. The valves are connected on the dorsal side by a strong elastic hinge or ligament which exerts a pulling action that separates the lower edges. This action is counteracted by one, or more commonly two, powerful cross muscles, called adductor muscles, which pull the two halves shut. If these muscles relax, the shell

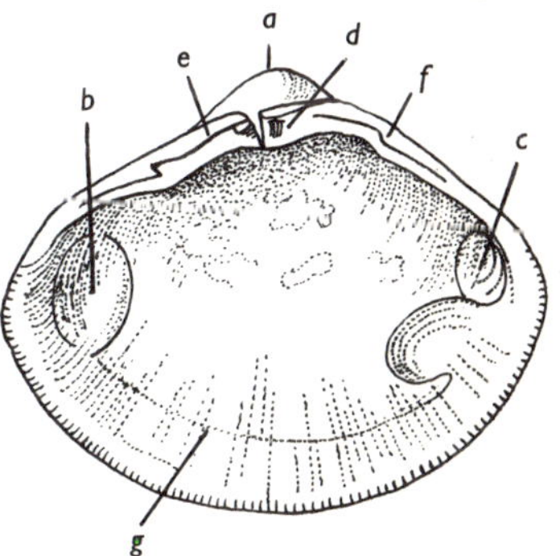

10. Inside of a bivalve shell:
a) beak b) point of attachment of the anterior adductor muscle
c) point of attachment of the posterior adductor muscle
d) cardinal tooth of the cardo
e), f) lateral teeth of the cardo
g) pallial line.

automatically opens. A dead bivalve can thus be easily distinguished from a live one by the fact that the shell does not close and the valves remain open when touched. Even in dead and empty shells one can see the points to which these muscles were attached in the form of mat oval or ovate impressions on the pearly inner surface of the valves. The shape of these impressions is so typical that it serves as a means of identification in some species.

The valves grow and enlarge at the outer open edges, where the free margins of the mantle continually secrete new shell layers. The oldest parts of each valve are raised and form the apex or beak. New layers are constantly added, which form distinct concentric growth lines on the surface. Unlike gastropods, however, the entire surface of the mantle of bivalves can secrete all three shell layers in case of need, thus enabling the animal to repair the shell whenever it is damaged.

Many specics of bivalves are able to produce pearls, which are formed when some foreign substance gets under the mantle where the smooth pearly layer is being deposited. A foreign substance that causes mechanical irritation of the mantle epithelium may be a grain of sand, or some similar substance. Such an object is encased by the animal in a special epithelial sac and then covered by numerous layers of mother-of-pearl. In pearl-bearing marine bivalves the formation of these pearls is often prompted by cysts or the larvae of parasitic trematodes and tapeworms, which the bivalve thereby renders harmless.

How Bivalves React to Environmental Stimuli

Because of their comparative inactivity and sedentary mode of life, with many bivalves spending most of the time buried in sand, the sensory organs are poorly developed. Within the mantle cavity bivalves have a pair of chemosensory organs, called **osphradia,** located at the base of the gills, and next to the pedal glands a pair of organs of equilibrium, called statocysts.

As we have already said, the head in this group of molluscs is greatly reduced and thus it is natural that the sensory organs normally found on the head are absent. There are no head tentacles or eyes in most species. The majority of bivalves are sensitive to light, however, which may be shown by the animal's vehement reaction when suddenly exposed to a strong beam of light. It should also be pointed out that many species which lead a more active life, such as the scallops and cockles, have a considerable number of eyes located on the fringes of the mantle (scallops) or at the edges of the siphons (cockles). Scallops have more than one hundred separate eyes of fairly complex structure. An interesting additional feature is the eyes of cockles which form clusters made up of a number of single eyes, something like the compound eyes of crustaceans and arthropods.

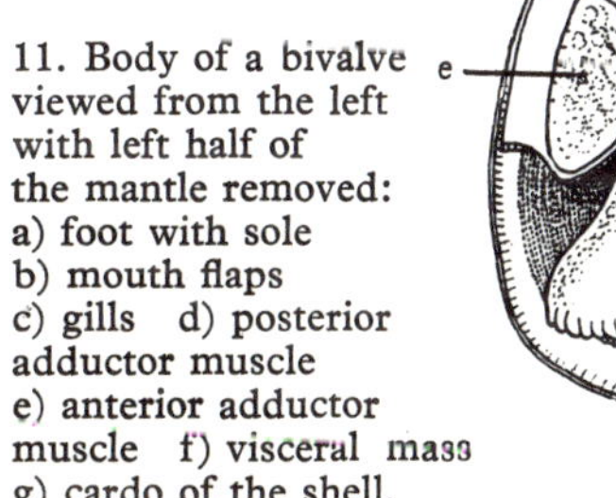

11. Body of a bivalve viewed from the left with left half of the mantle removed: a) foot with sole b) mouth flaps c) gills d) posterior adductor muscle e) anterior adductor muscle f) visceral mass g) cardo of the shell.

The tactile organs in bivalves are located around the mouth and on various kinds of tentacles, which in some species fringe the entire margin of the mantle. This great number and distribution of the tactile organs, vital for the more active species and their quick orientation, is a familiar characteristic, for example, of the scallops which flit rapidly through the water from one place to another. Tactile processes are also found at the openings of the siphons in bivalves that live buried in the sand and mud of the seabed.

Feeding and Digestion

Since bivalves have no head, certain parts of the digestive system normally located in the head are absent. There are no radula, teeth nor salivary glands. All that remains is the mouth, located on the base of the foot. Food reaches the mouth by a very complicated process. Small particles of food are brought into the gill chamber by the respiratory water, propelled to the gills by cilia. The action of the cilia gathers food particles, which are then covered with mucus and transported by other cilia to special appendages located around the mouth. On these appendages there are further rows of cilia which propel the food into the mouth, and from there to the stomach for digestion. Other groups of cilia create a reverse current of water travelling from or out of the mouth into the mantle cavity.

This method of feeding naturally does not allow any great selection of food and bivalves are truly not particular as to what they eat, though they are voracious feeders. All small particles pass through their stomach, be they digestible or not. In aquatic habitats, therefore, bivalves function as a sort of biological filter, clearing their environment of finely dispersed sediments and all impurities. The efficiency of such a filter is clearly evident from the fact that two oysters or edible mussels can clear the strongly muddied water of a large marine aquarium in a mere twenty-four hours. Because of their dependence on the plentiful supply of fine organic matter (plant and animal debris), marine bivalves are frequently found in places where sewage water flows into the sea, and it is the edible species such as mussels and oysters that often settle and multiply abundantly in harbours. Their vast numbers in the polluted waters of harbours make them a welcome and efficient biological filtering plant but at the same time present a serious health problem. With their voracious appetite they also filter from the water pathogenic micro-organisms such as typhoid bacteria. Mussels and oysters harvested in such places and then eaten raw or insufficiently cooked may become the source of widespread epidemics.

Pearls and their Formation

We have already mentioned the significance of molluscs, including bivalves, for man. Special interest, however, should be given to the importance of pearl-bearing molluscs. Pearls are found not only in pearl oysters but also in many other European marine bivalves such as edible oysters, pinnas, mussels, ear-shells, and the like. These, however, are small and of poor quality and therefore practically worthless. The most important world producer is the true Pearl Oyster *(Pinctada margaritifera)*, which has a thick mother-of-pearl lining in the shell. This oyster has a widespread geographical distribution extending from the Red Sea to the Pacific. It makes its home on hard substrata, generally at fairly shallow depths from one or two metres to fifteen or twenty metres. Only rarely does it descend to greater depths.

The breathtaking beauty of the pearls found inside the shell of this oyster has bewitched man for centuries. Pearls have been known and used as ornaments and currency since the dawn of man's history. Mention of precious pearls may be found in the oldest recorded Indian and Chinese documents of the forty-fifth to fortieth century BC. They are also mentioned in the Bible as well as in the works of ancient Greek and Roman writers. Pearls have been highly prized since ancient times, often even more than precious stones. According to Pliny, the Roman historian, the famous pearl of Queen Cleopatra was valued at half a million gold ducats (about two hundred thousand pounds). It is therefore not surprising that these lovely objects, fashioned by the hands of nature, kindled man's imagination, leading him to seek an explanation of their origin. The Brahmins were convinced that pearls were the materialization of the sun's morning rays. The ancient Romans' belief that pearls were of heavenly origin is testified to by the writings of Pliny. This otherwise realistic observer, one who had journeyed through the known world of that time, believed that the beauty of pearls was increased if the sky above the sea was clear and cloudless.

Man has understood the true origin of pearls for a long time, however, and the magic explanations have been left to tales and legends. The formation of a pearl by the Pearl Oyster is generally induced by the larva of the tapeworm *Tetrarhynchus unionifactor*, for which the oyster serves as an intermediate host, the adult form of this species living as a parasite in the intestine of the skate *(Raja)*. There the tapeworm also lays its eggs, which are passed into the seawater with the skate's excrement. The eggs are then filtered from the water by the Pearl Oyster along with other microscopic food particles. Once inside the body of this new host the larval parasite encysts itself, usually in the mantle of the mollusc. The ensuing mechanical irritation of the mantle causes it to envelop the foreign object, first with a porcellaneous layer and then with layer after layer of mother-of-pearl, until a pearl is formed. This concentric layering may be clearly seen on the crosscut section of a pearl.

As a rule the shape of the pearl corresponds to the shape of the nucleus or foreign body that has caused the irritation of the mantle and the pearl's subsequent formation. The size of pearls likewise shows marked variation. The smallest pearls are the size of a poppy seed and there may be several dozen of them in a single oyster. The largest pearls are generally pear-shaped (hence the common name 'tears of the sea') and may measure as much as three to four centimetres in length and two-and-a-half to three centimetres in width. A pearl usually has one nucleus, though pearls with several nuclei are not unknown. Because the pearl is generally located in a small sac formed by the mantle it is unattached. Occasionally, however, the pearl is cemented to the mother-of-pearl layer of the shell, thus naturally declining in value.

In the minds of most people pearls are white, or at best bluish or greyish. In reality, the coloration is extremely variable, ranging from white through various dark shades to black. Dark and black pearls are almost always formed at the edge of the mantle. A fairly general rule is that a pearl has the same colour as the mother-of-pearl layer of the oyster in which it was formed. The best known and most beautiful pure white pearls are obtained from the pearl oysters of Ceylon. Of all pearl oysters these are the smallest and their shells are also comparatively thin so that the mother-of-pearl layer is of little commercial value. Pearl oysters of the northern coast of Australia, on the other hand, are much larger and thicker and lined with a thick layer of mother-of-pearl. They rarely contain pearls, however, and when they do these are tinted a faint yellow and are less valuable than Ceylon pearls. The mother-of-pearl, however, is commercially processed on a wide scale. The pearl oysters collected in the Gulf of California and Gulf of Mexico off the coast of Central and North America have a grey or bronze-coloured mother-of-pearl layer and their pearls are darkly coloured to black. The oyster beds on the shores of Japan and Tahiti are very rich and profitable. Also famous are the beds on the shores of the Persian Gulf.

In most of the world's traditional pearl hunting grounds, as well as in smaller areas, pearl oysters are nowadays being cultivated artificially by a similar method to that used for edible oysters since ancient times. Productivity has been greatly increased by the 'inoculation' of the oysters with small artificial pearls inserted under the mantle. The inoculated animal continues to coat the foreign body with layers of mother-of-pearl, thus forming a new pearl. Each individual is marked with the date of inoculation and put into the sea at a designated point. Since pearl oysters are sedentary animals and anchor themselves firmly to a given spot by means of byssal threads, it is easy to keep a check on the formation of the pearls. The artificial cultivation of pearl oysters was introduced and developed first and foremost in Japan.

A pearl is actually a kind of miniature shell. The matter of which it is formed and its individual components are the same as those found in a shell. Besides the inorganic substances, calcium carbonate and aragonite, pearls also contain the organic component conchiolin. Despite their beauty and seeming firmness, pearls have one great disadvantage in that

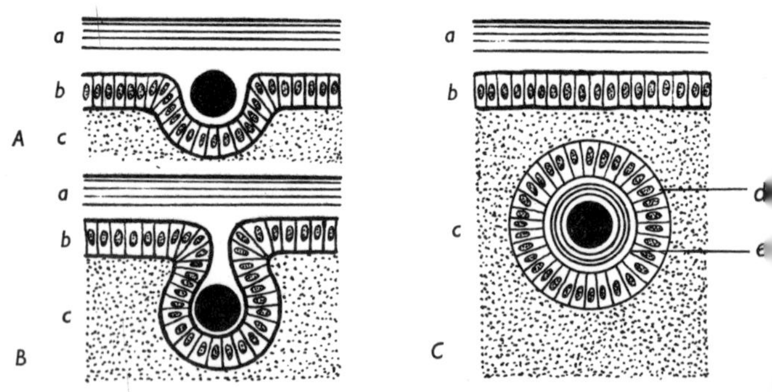

12. Diagram showing the formation of a pearl inside the shell of a bivalve:
A–C. stages of a pearl's growth a) mother-of-pearl layer of the shell b) epithelial cells of the mantle c) connective tissue of the mantle d) sac of epithelial cells of the mantle e) pearl.

their life is limited. In the course of time, changes in temperature as well as the corrosive effect of perspiration cause the natural pearl to lose the characteristic that makes it such a precious gem — its glowing pearly lustre — until it finally disintegrates completely. Pearls put in ancient graves as gifts to the deceased on their last journey bear testimony to the transient quality of earthly beauty, for all that now remains of them are tiny mounds of dust. Pearls dissolve after a time even in weak acid solutions because they contain up to ninety percent of calcium carbonate and all that remains is some insoluble sediment that forms the organic component of the pearl. Small pearls dissolve even in boiling vinegar.

The value of true pearls is comparable to that of precious stones and is therefore measured in terms of grains or quarter carats (one carat equals 0.2 grams). Of course the price of a pearl is not determined merely by its size and weight. Many other aspects are taken into account. The general evaluation of pearls is extremely difficult. In every specimen experts evaluate the shape, colour, lustre and weight, as well as various defects in the pearl. Perfectly spherical pearls are the most highly prized. Ones that are semi-spherical, button-shaped, pear-shaped or ovate are of lesser value and irregularly shaped ones are lowest on the scale. The appearance of a pearl and its purity depend, of course, on the fineness and regular formation of the mother-of-pearl layers, on the coloration and on various minor defects.

After having been thus evaluated every pearl is given a certain rating expressed in points ranging from 0 to 100. The final price is then determined by multiplying the square of its weight by the number of this rating.

CEPHALOPODA

Cephalopods, the most highly developed of all molluscs, far exceed the other members of this phylum in their body arrangement, physical abilities, development of the nervous system and powers governing their behaviour. The complexity and high degree of perfection of their body structure is evident at first glance. A layman lacking the necessary biological knowledge would hesitate to group these creatures, mostly excellent swimmers and in some cases predators dangerous even to man, together with other molluscs. Their internal body organization, however, proves this to be so.

Cephalopods are a very old group in geological time. Abundant evidence of their line is found in the oldest Silurian deposits. As early as the Paleozoic Era, cephalopods were so numerous and so widely distributed that the many members of this group became 'index fossils' of the Paleozoic layers of the Earth's crust. Today, about six hundred different species, all swift predatory creatures, inhabit the oceans of the world, but these are only a pitifully small remainder of the great wealth of genera and species of the past. Most are large animals, some growing to gigantic proportions and belonging to the largest creatures inhabiting our planet today.

External Shape and Internal Body Structure

The body of cephalopods is distinctly divided into a large head and sac-like trunk. The group takes its name, meaning 'head' and 'foot', from the fact that the two are so closely associated. The mouth, situated at the front of the head, is encircled by a ring of large muscular arms. These arms, which evolved from the front part of the foot, generally have the inner side covered with strong suckers that enable them to cling firmly to the substratum or to hold prey. Octopuses always have eight equally long arms. According to this distinguishing feature they are classed in a separate order (Octopoda). Another large group of cephalopods is the order Decapoda, which includes the familiar Common Cuttlefish *(Sepia officinalis)*, the Squid *(Loligo)*, and the largest known cephalopod – the Giant Squid *(Architeuthis dux)*, all possessing ten arms, two of which are always elongated and have spatulate tips. Only members of the genus *Nautilus* have a greater number of arms (up to ninety), but these are not equipped with suckers.

The suckers on the arms of cephalopods function on the basis of physical principles. The round, cartilaginous margin is firm but yet sufficiently elastic so that it can be pressed tightly to any surface. When the suckers have been applied to a surface the muscles lining the floor of the sucker contract, creating a vacuum which ensures firm attachment. The clinging power of these organs is so great that if an attempt is made to separate the animal from the object to which it is attached, often the arm itself is torn off rather than the sucker.

The mantle surrounds the entire body, forming a large mantle cavity on the underside of the trunk. Inside are the gills and the openings of internal organs. Water is brought into the mantle cavity through an opening below the head and forced out through a special funnel that can point forward or backward. Rhythmic contractions of muscles in the mantle draw water into the cavity and then force it out again. This exchange of water not only supplies oxygen to the gills but in many species also serves as a means of locomotion. When danger threatens the animal can forcibly eject such a powerful stream of water by rapidly contracting the muscles that it makes a sudden leap backward. Aiding greatly in deceiving and 'blinding' the enemy at such times is the cloud of brown 'ink' that the animal simultaneously ejects into the water.

The shell of most cephalopods is reduced, being well developed only in the members of the old genus *Nautilus*. In the remarkable pelagic species *Argonauta argo*, the female produces a very thin spiralled shell, secreted by a pair of arms and serving to protect the eggs. In other cephalopods the shell is either absent altogether or else is only a vestigial structure located under the skin on the back of the trunk.

The absence of a shell in the majority of cephalopods led to the development of an internal skeleton, which is unique not only in molluscs but in all invertebrates. The internal skeleton is made up of elastic cartilaginous connective tissue similar to the cartilage of vertebrates. This skeleton serves to protect the animal's nervous system and forms a structure analogous to the skull of vertebrates. Such cartilaginous structures are to be found also in other parts of a cephalopod's body.

Cephalopods are known for their ability to change colour with extreme rapidity. This is made possible by the chromatophores, large cells containing pigment, located in the skin, which change colour by expanding when irritated, thus making the colouring of the pigment more pronounced. Frequently the animals change their colour according to their surroundings.

The great mobility of cephalopods is made possible not only by the excellent internal coordination of the animal's functions but also by highly developed sensory organs. The most highly developed sense is sight. Except for the primitive *Nautilus*, the eyes of cephalopods are large enclosed sacs. They may be said to correspond to the eyes of vertebrates and possess a lens, cornea, iris and sometimes even lids. They are even capable of focusing on objects at varying distances. Compared to the size of the animal's body, the eyes of cephalopods are unusually large, especially in deep-sea forms, comprising from a half to twenty-five percent of the body weight and measuring up to forty centimetres in diameter.

HOW TO COLLECT SEASHELLS

Collecting interesting objects is a natural human activity. Of particular interest to collectors are attractive natural objects, mainly those that are easy to keep and that one can gather with one's own hands. In their way these objects then become 'hunter's trophies', which besides being valued for their intrinsic worth are treasured even more for the memories they call to mind – the magic of the day and place and the thrill of the moment when they were discovered. During the quiet hours spent poring over collections of such objects the collector is rewarded many times over for the time, money and effort devoted to his hobby.

Shells are just such objects – ones that have a number of features that make them worthwhile collectors' items. Most of them are very durable and do not require any special or continual care. At the same time their shape, surface sculpturing and coloration often make them extremely attractive. No less important is the fact that even a beginner can make a collection of shells with a comparatively small financial outlay and that one can acquire many interesting shells by collecting them oneself or trading with other collectors.

For these reasons shells were among the earliest objects to be collected. Extensive collections, organized on a scientific basis in line with the knowledge of that time, were made as early as the Middle Ages. The interest in these unusual natural objects was no doubt also prompted by the journeys and ocean voyages of discoverers, whereby Europeans came to be better acquainted with the remarkable beauty of tropical shells, their unusual shapes and bright, glowing colours. The growing number of admirers and collectors of shells naturally resulted in a greater demand for these objects accompanied by a rapid increase in their prices, especially of those species that were rare and difficult to obtain. Only the rich could afford to own such rarities, of course, and that holds true to this day. At special conchological exchanges, for instance, as much as three thousand pounds sterling has been known to be paid for certain rare species of cone shells.

The beginner who wishes to start a collection of sea shells would do best to start collecting specimens in suitable, easily reached localities. It is necessary to point out, however, that for those who wish to have a good collection it is not enough to gather empty shells cast up on the shore. These are generally greatly worn, damaged and smoothed by the pounding of the surf so that they are not suitable specimens for more serious study and comparison. If the collector wishes to acquire shells that are well-developed and at the same time damaged as little as possible he must seek out the living animals. If you do decide to collect the shells from living animals, it is important to ensure that the animal whose shell you have taken is not left to suffer a slow death. It is also essential that you do not collect more than is absolutely necessary. Depleting the species in a particular area can sometimes have serious ecological consequences.

A great many species of marine molluscs are to be found between the high and low tide marks and can thus be gathered with comparative ease on the exposed shore when the tide is out. On rocky shores the collector must remember to look carefully not only for the various molluscs that cling firmly to the rock surfaces but also for those concealed in crevices and under stones. Many species live permanently embedded in the sand and mud of the seabed and are rarely to be found on the surface. It is therefore necessary to dig up spadefuls of mud and sand with a suitable implement and wash this through in a sieve with a metal or nylon mesh. The size of the mesh depends on the size of the shells the collector is looking for. Those who wish to acquire the shells of molluscs inhabiting greater depths have no other recourse than to obtain diving equipment and set out to discover the beauties of the submarine world. This is a very interesting and exciting method of hunting. One can descend to fairly great depths and remain there for some time, during which one sees many interesting things. Diving, however, may be very dangerous for an inexperienced swimmer and therefore should be attempted only under the watchful eye and guidance of a skilled companion or after a thorough training such as is offered by various sporting clubs.

After being brought home the shells must be properly prepared and preserved for the collection. First of all it is necessary to remove the soft fleshy parts. Bivalves are easily killed by putting them in warm fresh water. The shells of the dead animal soon gape and the body can be removed by cutting the adductor muscles with a knife. Then the shells must be thoroughly cleaned, the valves closed and then fastened together with thread or a rubber band. The shells must be dried slowly in a shady and well-ventilated spot, for if dried in strong sun they become fragile and break easily. Gastropods can likewise be killed by putting them in water which is then heated, after which the animal is taken out of the shell, all fleshy remnants are removed and the empty shell thoroughly washed out with the aid of a syringe. Small shells may be put in seventy percent alcohol for a few weeks and then cleaned and dried.

Fragile and thin shells may become overdry after a time and develop cracks. This may be prevented by coating them with vaseline or impregnating them with glycerine. The colour pattern can be brightened by spreading nut oil or other vegetable fat over the surface. This also increases the shells' resistance to external factors such as dampness and dryness.

Individual specimens are usually put in separate boxes and may be covered with a glass lid. Small and delicate specimens are best stored in tightly closed éprouvettes (test tubes), which may be put in individual boxes in the usual way. If the shell has a calcareous or horny lid (operculum), as is usually the case in prosobranchs, this should be glued back in place or else on a piece of cardboard beside the shell. The second method is better. Larger boxes may be used to store several specimens of the same species, but these must be from the same locality and gathered on the same date.

If the collection is to have any documentary and scientific value each shell must be provided with identity and locality labels on which are recorded the date and method of collection, the place and habitat and the collector's name. If the shell has been identified then the Latin name of the species as well as the common name should be recorded on the identity label, also the name of the family to which it belongs. Naturally, the name of the person who identified it should be recorded here, too.

Shell collections are not endangered by pests but may be damaged by extreme changes in temperature and humidity, and by direct illumination, and must therefore be stored in a fairly dry and unheated room. Individual specimens, as well as sets of similar specimens, should be stored in related groups, e.g. members of a single genus or family in larger boxes, which are then put in cabinets adapted for this purpose.

A well-kept, classified and labelled collection will give pleasure to all who view it. It will also have scientific value, particularly in these days of rapid industrial development, which often result in changes in the natural environment.

PLATES

Coat-of-mail Shells

Chitonidae

Chiton olivaceus **SPENGLER**

Chiton olivaceus is one of the most primitive existing molluscs. This is borne out not only by the body structure and internal arrangement but also by the primitive type of larva.

The shell, which covers only the animal's upper surface, attains a length of 30—40 mm. It is quite unusual in construction and differs from the shells of other molluscs in that it consists of a series of eight convex plates that articulate and overlap much like the tiles of a roof. They enable the animal to curl up when danger threatens.

The shells are extremely variable in colour, and may be yellow-brown to olive-grey; sometimes also black, red, orange or yellow. On the upper surface they have transverse as well as longitudinal stripes. The second and seventh plates are usually of a different colour. This mollusc lives firmly attached to stones and rocks in the splash zone. It feeds on minute algae that form a surface film on rocks.

Lepidochitona cinereus LINNÉ

Lepidochitona cinereus is a smaller species, about 12 mm long. Its shell is not as colourful and is generally green or brown. Its mode of life and habitat is similar to that of *Chiton olivaceus*. It is probably the commonest chiton on the shores of Great Britain.

Chiton olivaceus 1
Lepidochitonia cinereus 2

1

2

Sea Ear or **Ormer** Haliotidae

Haliotis tuberculata LINNÉ

Haliotis tuberculata belongs to a group of very primitive gastropod molluscs. The shell is flat and shallow, the whorls widening so abruptly that the overall effect is that of a human ear. This resemblance is the reason not only for the animal's scientific name but also for the name by which it is known in the various languages, e.g. 'Orechia di San Pietro' (Ear of St Peter) in Italian and 'Sea Eaı' in English.

The exterior of the shell is dark grey with dark brown marbling and distinct transverse and longitudinal grooves. Inside it is lined with a thick layer of mother-of-pearl. At the outer edge are a series of holes through which the exhalent current escapes.

H. tuberculata is abundant in the European seas, especially in the Mediterranean. It is commonly found in the littoral zone, where it adheres firmly to rocks, the underside of stones, harbour constructions, and the like. It feeds on the algal covering of rocks.

In the Mediterranean it is commonly gathered for the valuable mother-of-pearl, used in making fancy goods and souvenirs. In the Channel Islands it is also gathered for food.

Diodora italica DEFRANCE — Fissurellidae

Diodora italica has a fairly firm shell shaped like a small bowl and grows to a length of 60 mm. The surface is marked with a very rugged network pattern made up of radiating ribs of varying thickness crossed by finer transverse ribs. Viewed from the top it is possible to see the stages of the animal's growth. The apex of the shell is located somewhat nearer the rear end; it is truncated and terminated by an elongate hole. The colour is comparatively variable, generally yellowish-grey with eight greyish-violet concentric rings.

This limpet lives on the stony bottom of the littoral zone but is not as hardy as members of the genus *Patella;* it does not tolerate even a short period out of water. For this reason it is usually found at a depth of about ten metres where the ebb tide is no longer felt.

Emarginula huzardi PAYRAUDEAU

Emarginula huzardi has a fairly small (about 20 mm), thick shell, also shaped like a small bowl. It is readily identified by the slit-like opening in the front margin of the shell. The exterior has a distinct network pattern of thick and thinner radiating ribs crossed by spiral grooves and ridges. The ground colour is generally white. This limpet is found in large numbers on the rocky bottom of the littoral zone at shallow depths, generally under stones. It feeds on the film of seaweed covering the rocks.

Diodora italica 1
Emarginula huzardi 2

1

2

This medium-sized limpet has a flat, roundish-oval shell measuring up to 30–40 mm in length and marked with a large number of irregular radiating ribs and distinct growth lines. The colour is fairly variable, ranging from reddish-brown to grey, often covered with white spots or radiating lines.

Patella coerulea inhabits the splash zone. The irregular margin of the shell is so adapted to the substratum that it permits the limpet to adhere firmly to the rocky bottom even if the surface is irregular. At low tide the animal is left high and dry for hours at a time and is often exposed to strong sunshine.

Although it moves about in search of food at night, *P. coerulea* always returns to the same part of the rock. It feeds on the minute vegetation that covers rocks, continually rasping a thin layer off with the radula as it slowly moves along. Its method of feeding may be observed very well on the walls of an aquarium filled with such seaweed.

P. coerulea is a very common edible species widely distributed on European coasts, throughout the Mediterranean and as far as the Aegean Sea and Sea of Marmara.

Common Limpet

Patellidae

Patella vulgata **LINNÉ**

Patella vulgata has a low conical shell growing to a length of 60 mm. The outer surface bears rugged radiating ridges and is generally tinted green or brown. The interior has a glossy nacreous appearance with alternate white and dark brown rays.

This limpet inhabits the littoral zone, where it clings firmly to rocks and stones. Because of its irregular margin the shell is able to cling to surfaces that have minor distortions. Great force is required to pry it loose. The limpet is very hardy; it may even remain out of water for a short time, e.g. when the tide ebbs, and endure dilution of its surroundings with fresh water during rains. It leaves its habitat only at night to feed on the film of plant material growing on rocks. Most remarkable of the limpet's habits is that it returns to its 'home base' after each excursion with the break of dawn. It inhabits all the European seas and is an edible species.

Blue-rayed Limpet

Patina (Acmaea) pellucida **LINNÉ**

Patina pellucida grows to a height of only 20 mm. The markedly convex shell resembles a Phrygian cap. The exterior is smooth and coloured brown with bright blue lines radiating from the apex to the margin. Unlike other limpets, this species lives upon seaweed and not on stones.

Patella vulgata 1
Patina pellucida 2

2

1

Gibbula adansoni Payraudeau

Gibbula adansoni has a conical shell measuring up to 13.5 mm in height and 12.5 mm in breadth, and is composed of six to seven slightly convex whorls separated by a deep suture. The outer surface bears slightly convex spiral ridges. The colour is variable; the ground colour is pale yellow to reddish, with irregular dark-brown and white rays, often separated by one to two reddish lines.

It is found in large numbers in the upper regions of the littoral zone, often on stones among broken shell remnants and also on seaweed. It is widely distributed in the Mediterranean, the Black Sea and has even spread to the Sea of Azov.

Gibbula albida Gmelin

Gibbula albida is a medium-large species, the shell growing to a height of 21 mm and a breadth of 23 mm. It has six to seven whorls with a fairly prominent ledge below the suture. The slightly rounded, flat, spiral ridges are separated by broad, smooth bands. The colour is variable, ranging from pale yellow or greenish to dark brown, overlaid with white marbling and brown, red and grey dots, streaks and spots.

It inhabits the whole of the Mediterranean, where it is found on stones and among seaweed.

Gibbula adansoni 1
Gibbula albida 2

1

2

Great Topshell

Trochidae

Gibbula magus **Linné**

Gibbula magus is a medium-sized gastropod mollusc, the shell measuring only 20 – 30 mm across. It is conical, with seven whorls separated by a deep suture. These do not fit tightly together on the central shaft thus giving rise to a distinct, hollow umbilicus. In the living animal the mouth of the shell is closed with a horny lid, or operculum. The surface has a puckered appearance, caused by a great number of fine spiral ribs. This mollusc can be identified by the row of knobs at the top of each whorl.

The coloration of the shell is very rich and exhibits marked variation. The ground colour is yellowish-white with irregular, zig-zag, radiating streaks of red. The inside of the shell is a beautiful pearly white with red lines shining through.

G. magus is commonly found in great numbers on all types of seabeds in the littoral and adjacent deeper zone, but must be looked for at depths of more than ten metres. The empty shells, however, may often be found cast up on the shore.

Painted Topshell

Trochidae

Calliostoma zizyphinum LINNÉ

Calliostoma zizyphinum has a pointed conical shell growing to a height of 40 mm. The surface of the first whorls is granular, the remaining whorls are partly smooth and partly covered with spiral lines.

Members of this genus are noted for the beautiful coloration and fine pattern of the shell. *C. zizyphinum* is a true gem, coloured reddish-yellow to white dotted with red spots, though one may also come across wine-red individuals.

It is found on soft muddy and sandy bottoms, often among seaweed. It feeds on polyps.

Variegated Topshell

Gibbula divaricata LINNÉ

Gibbula divaricata is related to the above species. It is of medium size, up to 23 mm in height and 19 mm in breadth. The shell is tapering, conical and has six inflated whorls. The first few are smooth, the others have a large number of spiral ridges of various sizes. The ground colour is greenish-yellow, with a network of radiating lines composed of carmine-red spots. This species is found in abundance in the stony littoral zone under stones or among seaweed, on which it feeds.

Calliostoma zizyphinum 1
Gibbula divaricata 2

1
2

Monodonta articulata Lamarck — Trochidae

Monodonta articulata has a very thick, tall, conical shell, composed of six to seven whorls. It grows up to 50 mm in height and 42 mm in diameter. The whorls are separated by a shallow suture. The mouth of the shell is broadly oval, smooth on the outside and with a characteristic, strong, prominent tooth inside. The shell surface is almost smooth but has spiral sculpturing, which in some cases may be very distinct, as for instance, on the uncovered mother-of-pearl layer of the oldest whorls.

The shell is very colourful with marked variations in the colouring. The ground colour may be rose or grey to greenish. It is ornamented with a dense network of wavy and zig-zag reddish-brown to brownish-black lines and stripes that follow a roughly radiating course. This pattern is overlaid with several paler brown spiral bands.

M. articulata is a common inhabitant of rocky coasts, chiefly in the splash zone. It is also common on stone harbour constructions just below the low water mark. The strong shell, closed by a hard, calcareous operculum, will stand up to even the strongest pounding of the waves and the animal can also tolerate a brief period out of water at ebb tide.

Clanculus cruciatus LINNÉ — Trochidae

Clanculus cruciatus is a small but very attractive gastropod with a thick, rounded, slightly conical shell, about as wide as it is high (10 mm). There are five whorls, the first of which is smooth, the others marked with five to six granulated spiral lines. The last two whorls are markedly convex. The coloration is rufous-brown to dark brown and each whorl bears four white spots below the suture. The concentric ribs on the underside of the shell round the umbilicus are alternately striped brown and white.

C. cruciatus is commonly found beneath stones and among the seaweed of the rock shores of the Mediterranean and southern Atlantic.

Mitrella scripta LINNÉ — Anachidae

The spindle-shaped shell of *Mitrella scripta* is composed of eight to nine whorls each successively larger than the preceding one and all connecting closely with one another, separated by only a shallow suture. The shell grows to a height of approximately 15 mm and a width of 6 mm. The siphonal canal is broad, straight and short. The surface of the shell is plain.

The ground colour may be white, rufous or brown, marked with a pattern of darker irregular lines and spots. The inside of the mouth is yellow or brownish.

M. scripta inhabits the Atlantic coast of southern Europe and is found throughout the whole of the Mediterranean, usually on hard bottoms and among vegetation.

Clanculus cruciatus 1
Mitrella scripta 2

1
2

Turban Shell

Turbinidae

Tricolia pulla LINNÉ

Tricolia pulla has an attractive shell with a heavy calcareous operculum closing the aperture when the animal is alive. It only grows to a height of 8 – 9 mm. Examination through a magnifying glass reveals a pattern of spiral lines composed of numerous small red dots. The ground colour is brown, yellow or rose. The spiral lines are supplemented by black and white flame-shaped markings. *T. pulla* is found in large numbers on sandy bottoms in the littoral zone, often also on seaweed. It feeds on the surface film of plant material growing on rocks and on organic debris.

The small shells are very durable and far outlast the animals that have formed them. They are washed up by the sea in vast numbers on to the sandy shore and whole layers of them may be found washed up between rocks. They are used in making necklaces and bracelets.

Tricolia speciosa MÜHLFELD

Tricolia speciosa has a shell that is somewhat larger and narrower, growing to a height of about 13 mm. The lid closing the aperture is ovate, thickened and rounded on the outside. The whorls (four to five) are markedly convex and separated by a deep suture. The ground colour is generally rose to yellow with white spiral bands composed of lines and spots.

It is also a common species of the littoral zone, found mostly on sandy bottoms and among seaweed growing on rocks. Strings of these shells are popular as jewellery.

Tricolia pulla 1
Tricolia speciosa 2

1
2

Astraea rugosa Linné Turbinidae

The shell of this mollusc is large, very strong and thick, and grows to about 55 mm in height and 60 mm in diameter. There are seven whorls separated by a deep suture. On the upper edge of each whorl there is a row of thick, spiny processes. Beneath these are rows of granulated spiral bands divided by ridges marking the growth lines, often bearing scale-like processes. The aperture is markedly convex with a sharp margin, and is closed by a thick operculum. The shell is very colourful. At the top the colour ranges from brown to green marked with large irregular spots, at the bottom it is a bright orange-red. The convex operculum is the same colour. The inside of the mouth glows with pearly hues.

The shell as a whole has a very bizarre look. To Italian fishermen it has always been known as 'Occhio de Santa Lucia' (the eye of Santa Lucia).

Astraea rugosa lives on hard rocky bottoms of the littoral and sublittoral zone. Its distribution is regular but nowhere is it found in large numbers.

It inhabits the Mediterranean and the south-west European coast of the Atlantic. In some places it is gathered for food. The decorative shells are often used to make ornamental objects.

Periwinkle or **Common European Winkle**

Littorinidae

Littorina littorea LINNÉ

The shell of this species is up to 30 mm high, thick, ovate and with a pointed apex. There are six to seven only slightly rounded whorls. The surface bears the characteristic sculpture of rugged spiral lines crossed with the transverse growth bands. The colour is quite variable, generally greyish with brown lines and bands.

Littorina littorea lives in the upper regions of the littoral zone, often in the tidal zone, on sea vegetation, stones and harbour constructions. At low tide the animal withdraws into its firm shell and closes the aperture with an operculum. It can live for some time out of water, frequently foraging for food on dry land. This is made possible by its having reduced gills and the mantle lining richly supplied with blood capillaries, which enable the animal to absorb oxygen from the air.

L. littorea feeds on seaweed and organic debris. It is widely distributed along the European coast of the Atlantic and is of great commercial value for it is an edible species that is very popular and widely gathered, especially in England.

Small Periwinkle or **Nerite Winkle** Littorinidae

Littorina neritoides LINNÉ

The shell of *Littorina neritoides*, growing to a height of 6 mm, is spherical with five whorls, the last of which is strongly inflated. The surface is without the spiral sculpturing. The coloration is fairly variable, ranging from dark brown to violet with white to blue spots below the margin of the last whorl.

This is a common species of the splash zone of rocky coasts, often occurring on rocks among growths of blue-green algae up to ten metres above the level of the water surface. In its strong shell with the aperture closed by the operculum, it is remarkably resistant to desiccation. It is also very tolerant of changes in the salinity of water.

The diet consists chiefly of the film of seaweed growing on rocks in the splash zone. Often this winkle occurs in such vast numbers that the rocks look as if they were covered with thousands of small marbles. In *L. neritoides* the sexes are separate. The eggs are fertilized inside the body of the female and are released singly. They are not discharged all at once but in batches, enclosed in a protective egg case, the peak period being during the winter months.

L. neritoides is very widespread. It is found on the Atlantic coast from North Africa to the North Sea as well as throughout the Mediterranean and even in the Black Sea.

Rissoa variabilis MÜHLFELD

Rissoa variabilis is a typical representative of the family Rissoidae, which consists of small to minute species of prosobranchs with very variable shells. The shell is an elongated ovate cone up to 10 mm high and 4.5 mm across, composed of nine inflated whorls marked with prominent radiating ridges. The colour is milky white, sometimes tinged greenish-yellow, and ornamented with many variable brown spiral lines.

It is regularly found in large numbers among growths of seaweed and is also plentiful on submarine meadows.

Alvania cimex LINNÉ

The genus *Alvania* is closely related to *Rissoa* and belongs to the same family. The shell of *Alvania cimex* is a strong ovate cone composed of seven slightly inflated whorls, attaining a height of 6 mm and a breadth of 4.5 mm. The surface of the thick shell is marked with regular sculpturing consisting of a dense and distinctive mosaic composed of small knobs. The spiral ribs are also well developed on the inside wall of the final whorl.

The shell is generally unicoloured, ranging from white to brownish. Only in rare instances are there one or two darker spiral lines.

This species is widespread in the Mediterranean.

Rissoa variabilis 1
Alvania cimex 2

1

2

Auger or **European Screw Shell** Turritellidae

Turritella communis Risso

The shell of *Turritella communis* is sharply pointed and turret-shaped, and attains a length of 50 mm and a breadth of 15 mm. It has a large number (fourteen to nineteen) of rounded whorls separated by a shallow suture. The aperture is closed by a horny operculum.

The surface is marked by spiral ridges of various sizes. As a rule three to five of the ridges are more rugged, the remaining six to nine are finer. The colour is variable, ranging from reddish-violet to rose, sometimes white, often with brown streaks.

T. communis is a widespread species found in large numbers on muddy, sandy and gravelly bottoms, mostly at depths of ten to forty metres, though it descends to depths of about two hundred metres.

The diet consists of small seaweed and particles of animal debris which are filtered from the water passing through the gills. The stream of water propelled inside the shell by lashing cilia serves a three-fold purpose. It brings oxygen to the gills, carries off gaseous waste products and at the same time ensures a continual supply of food.

This species is widespread throughout the Atlantic, the Mediterranean and neighbouring parts of the Black Sea.

Triphora perversa Linné Triphoridae

Unlike most other gastropod molluscs *Triphora perversa* has a shell with sinistral or left-handed coiling, as its scientific name indicates. Narrow and turret-shaped, it grows to a height of 30 mm and a breadth of 4 mm, although British specimens are much smaller, only about 7 mm high by 2 mm broad. The long cone is composed of a fairly large number of flat whorls, usually twelve to fourteen, separated by a shallow suture. At the mouth of the shell is a short, curved siphonal canal.

The shell exhibits very attractive markings. The whorls are covered with spiral ridges consisting of pearl-like knobs set close to one another. The upper whorls have double rows of these knobs. The colour of the shell is reddish-brown to light brown.

This species is found in the stony regions of the rocky littoral zone, where it generally conceals itself under stones. It descends below this zone to depths of about eighty metres.

T. perversa has a widespread geographic distribution, inhabiting the European coast of the Atlantic, as far north as Norway. It is native to the whole of the Mediterranean and is fairly plentiful even on the west and north coasts of the Black Sea.

Lemintina arenaria LINNÉ Vermetidae

Lemintina arenaria begins its life with a normal spiral shell. Later, however, it cements the shell to the object on which it is lodged and it turns into an irregularly coiled tube. The last whorl is straight and uncoiled. The diameter of the shell may be 10 – 15 mm and the surface is marked with numerous spiral lines. The colour is a drab greyish-yellow.

L. arenaria leads a sedentary life, pressed close to the stony bed or to corals. This has led to marked changes in its body structure. The foot has degenerated except for the small horny operculum. A remainder of the original foot is the large mucus gland which plays an important role in gathering food, which the firmly attached and immovable mollusc obtains in quite an interesting way. The mouth of its shell points straight up. The animal is sensitive to any movement of water caused by the passage of its prey, and when this happens the gland secretes three to four filaments of mucus extending upward to a length of thirty centimetres. Tiny animals as well as seaweed and organic debris floating in the water are caught on these filaments and then pulled back into the animal's mouth.

Cerithium vulgatum Bruguière Cerithiidae

Cerithium vulgatum is a robust species. The broadly turret-shaped, strong, thick shell reaches a height of 60 mm and a breadth of 19 mm. There are fourteen to fifteen slightly convex whorls pressed close to each other, their surface marked with a rugged pattern. On the larger whorls in the middle of the shell the tubercles and larger knobs covering the shell surface are arranged in three spiral rows, the roughest ones in the middle row. The last whorl bears several further rows of smaller knobs. Besides these tubercles and knobs the entire surface is marked with a large number of spiral grooves and small ridges. The mouth is broadly oval with a short siphonal canal in the centre.

The ground colour of the shell is reddish-yellow with irregular radial streaks and spots that form a changing pattern. The knobs are brown and white, the mouth white outside and spotted brown inside.

C. vulgatum is common on stony and firm sandy bottoms, often on oyster banks, where it rasps the seaweed that covers rocks and other hard objects. Even more plentiful than the live animals are the empty shells found in shallow water or washed up on the shore. The strong, thick walls make these shells very durable.

Cerithium rupestre RISSO Cerithiidae

Another representative of the genus *Cerithium*, whose members are noted for their very ornamental shells, is *Cerithium rupestre*. It is much smaller than *Cerithium vùlgatum*, the shell reaching about 25 mm in length and 10 mm in breadth. It too is composed of a large number of whorls, the last ones being distinctly convex, and the mouth with a short siphonal canal is similarly broadened.

The surface pattern and coloration of *C. rupestre* are just as distinctive as in *C. vulgatum*. Each individual whorl bears two spiral rows of smaller knobs and the entire surface is finely grooved and covered with low spiral ribs.

The ground colour may be whitish-yellow, yellow-green to brown, with brown wavy lines and dots. The knobs are white.

C. rupestre is a very plentiful species commonly found in the upper regions of the littoral zone of the Mediterranean. It is especially abundant among the marine vegetation of rocky shores and is always found at shallow depths. It feeds on the vegetation that covers rocks and other solid substrata.

Small Needle Whelk

Cerithiidae

Bittium reticulatum da Costa

This species is a representative of a genus distinguished by slender ovate shells, the coils ornamented with tubercled spiral lines. The mouth, notched at the bottom, is closed by an oval operculum. *Bittium reticulatum* possesses all these characteristics and it also bears a marked resemblance both in general appearance and surface pattern to the two members of the genus *Cerithium* described in this book. The anatomical and morphological structure of the animal also bear out the close relationship between the two genera.

B. reticulatum is a small species, the shell reaching a length of only 12 mm. There is a large number of slightly convex whorls separated by a deep suture. A large number of radial tubercles crossed by four spiral bands form a regular network pattern which makes the shell extremely attractive despite the fact that it is a uniform dark brown.

B. reticulatum is common among growths of seaweed on rocky bottoms. It is also abundant on soft bottoms and among the vegetation of submarine meadows.

Common Wentletrap

Scalidae

Clathrus clathrus LINNÉ

Clathrus clathrus has a turret-shaped shell with a large number (twelve to fifteen) of markedly convex whorls, regularly increasing in size and separated by a deep suture. Often they do not even touch. The exterior of the shell is strengthened by ridges that regularly cross each whorl, joining vertically to form almost continuous bands. The shell is about 30 mm high and 12 mm in diameter. The aperture is closed by an operculum. The colour is very delicate, usually white or pale pink, the bands are sometimes reddish or marked with horizontal streaks. The loose coiling, unusual surface sculpturing and pale coloration make the shell look like a piece of alabaster filigree work. Large tropical species were at one time highly valued and sold for fantastic prices.

C. clathrus is a predatory gastropod mollusc. It is found on sandy and muddy bottoms, often at depths of as much as one hundred metres. It has a scattered distribution, however, and does not reproduce in large numbers.

Its home is the Mediterranean and the west European coast of the Atlantic, its range extending northward as far as the North Sea.

Turton's Wentletrap

Scalidae

Clathrus turtonis TURTON

The shell of *Clathrus turtonis* is similar to that of the closely related *Clathrus communis*. It is a very elongate cone composed of twelve to fourteen distinctly convex and regularly coiled whorls, separated by a fairly deep suture. It measures up to 43 mm in length and 13 mm in width.

The surface is decorated with a pattern of faint, narrow grooves. Each whorl is crossed by eight to ten ridges, some of which are connected from whorl to whorl to form a continuous line. The mouth is oval with a thickened, recurved lip, which is actually formed by the last of the ridges, and is closed by a dark brown operculum.

The shell is generally coloured a brownish hue, sometimes with a faint pattern of dark brown spiral lines. The ridges are similarly coloured but somewhat lighter.

C. turtonis lives on stony and sandy bottoms, being partial to coral beds. It is found at depths of ten to eighty metres. Its range of distribution extends from the Black Sea throughout the Mediterranean and on to the European coast of the Atlantic northward as far as the shores of Great Britain.

The shell of *Janthina fragilis* is very thin, transparent, and coloured bluish-violet. Even though delicate and fragile it provides, with the animal's unusual way of life, a sufficient protection against its enemies. *J. fragilis* is a pelagic species, drifting freely over the surface of the sea, where it floats with the aid of a kind of raft resembling a mass of foam. This consists of bubbles of air imprisoned in hardened slime secreted by mucus glands in the animal's foot. *J. fragilis* fabricates these air bubbles by extending the front end of the foot (which is shaped like a horn) to the surface, filling it with air, and then pulling the bubble under water and enveloping it in a coat of mucus. Six to ten of these bubbles are then stuck to each other and the creature proceeds in this way until it has fabricated an entire raft measuring up to twelve centimetres in length and two centimetres in width, to the underside of which it attaches its eggs. The female lays a total of some two and a half million eggs placed in five hundred capsules.

J. fragilis is a predatory species that feeds on floating plankton, its most frequent prey being planktonic coelenterates, which it often swallows whole. It is also known to eat members of its own species.

Hungarian Cap

Capulidae

Capulus ungaricus LINNÉ

The body structure and formation of the shell of this species is typical of the family, and has many remarkable features. The shell is conical with the apex spirally curled back and inward. The mouth is wider than it is long, measuring up to 50 mm across. The shell surface bears numerous radiating lines shaped like ribs which are crossed by the shallow transverse growth lines. The outer horny layer covered with fine hairs is felt-like to the touch.

The colour of the shell is variable. The exterior is whitish-yellow or pink to brown; the inside mother-of-pearl layer a gleaming white.

The unusual shape, reminiscent of a medieval Hungarian cap, prompted the famous naturalist Linnaeus to give it the Latin name under which it is classified.

C. ungaricus is found on all hard seabeds of the littoral zone, firmly attached to the substratum. When young, it occasionally moves from one place to another but when adult it does not abandon its chosen home unless forced to do so. It feeds on small algae and organic debris which it strains from the water.

Slipper Limpet

Calyptraeidae

Crepidula fornicata LINNÉ

Crepidula fornicata has a low shell resembling a large button. The last whorl forms the largest part of the shell, which is up to 47 mm wide and 20 mm high. The surface is coloured whitish-yellow to brown, with darker, irregular radiating lines.

C. fornicata is a native North American species, brought to England with oysters in 1880, whence it subsequently spread to the continental coast and now occurs in such numbers that it has become a pest of oyster beds, killing the oysters by smothering them as well as competing with them for food.

This species is hermaphroditic. When young, when it is mobile, it produces male cells; later it attaches itself to a solid object, becomes sterile and eventually lays eggs. The animals live in piles or chains of as many as twelve individuals. These chains are formed by young animals settling successively one after the other upon a large old female. The lowest individuals in the chain are females, the top individuals males and those in the middle of the chain are sterile individuals.

Chinaman's Hat

Calyptraea chinensis LINNÉ

Calyptraea chinensis has a small, thin, low, conical shell measuring up to 29 mm in diameter and 7 mm in height. The colour is a milky white.

It lives attached to solid objects and is widespread along the eastern and western coasts of the Atlantic, in the Mediterranean and in the Black Sea.

Crepidula fornicata 1
Calyptraea chinensis 2

1

2

Pelican's Foot

Aporrhaidae

Aporrhais pespelecani LINNÉ

Aporrhais pespelecani is one of the commonest of European gastropod molluscs. The shell is thick and firm, up to 55 mm high and 45 mm wide. In older individuals the lip is thickened and expanded into a broad flap with three to five finger-like processes resembling, as the scientific name indicates, the foot of a pelican. The shell has ten to twelve convex whorls and the colour may be white, yellow, pale pink, or greenish to grey; the mouth of the shell is pale yellow.

A. pespelecani lives in large numbers on various types of seabeds as well as on hard sandy ground, generally at depths of ten metres or more. The unusual shape of the shell is very well adapted to its peculiar way of life and feeding. Using the toothed shell to plough along in the sand or mud it feeds on the remnants of plant and animal matter it finds there.

It is found on the European coast of the Atlantic, its distribution extending northward as far as Iceland. It is also widespread in the Mediterranean.

The firm and beautifully coloured shell is used in making ornaments and souvenirs.

Common Necklace Shell

Naticidae

Natica catena DA COSTA

Natica catena has a very strong, oval shell measuring up to 30 mm in height and about the same in diameter. There are six to seven whorls pressed close together. The ground colour is yellowish, with irregular, very variable markings consisting of a series of zig-zag reddish-brown stripes and spots.

When the animal crawls through the sand the head and front part of the shell are protected by a fold of the foot. The proboscis has a special gland secreting an acid which softens the shells of its victims.

N. catena is found on muddy bottoms, intertidally, or at greater depths. It uses the front part of the foot as a plough blade to cut through the mud. It is a merciless predator of other molluscs. It envelops the victim with its foot and presses the proboscis tightly to the shell of its prey. Then, with the aid of the secretion produced by the proboscidean gland, and with the radula, it bores a hole about one to two millimetres in diameter in the shell, the whole process taking up to several hours. Then it extends its ten millimetre long proboscis through the hole and with the radula eats the fleshy parts of the animal. Such drilled shells may often be found washed up on the shore in large numbers.

Natica millepunctata LAMARCK Naticidae

This species has an oval shell, measuring up to 35 mm in height, with a massive final whorl and mouth the shape of a half-moon. The individual whorls are separated by a suture and resemble shallow steps. The ground colour is white, changing to grey towards the middle of the whorls and orange-yellow towards the apex. The mouth is white. The entire surface is covered with numerous brownish-red, oval spots arranged in irregular radiating lines.

This predatory gastropod mollusc lives on sandy and muddy bottoms at greater depths. It uses its greatly enlarged and swollen foot as a plough to burrow along in the sand and mud in search of food. If it encounters a bivalve it wraps its foot around its victim and drills the shell in the same way as *Natica catena* – by chemical action and with the radula, thereupon eating the soft fleshy parts inside.

Natica has an unusual method of protecting itself from its chief enemy, the starfish. At the merest touch of the starfish *Asterias rubens*, it immediately covers its entire shell with the greatly enlarged and swollen foot and the slippery surface then prevents the starfish from attaching itself with the sucking action of its tube feet. This simple method of defence is very effective because the starfish will not begin eating its prey until it has obtained a firm hold. The snail is thus able to flee from its reach.

Lurid Cowrie

Cypraeidae

Luria lurida LINNÉ

Luria lurida has a somewhat unusual shell, in which the final whorl covers all the preceding ones. The aperture is a long narrow slit with a toothed margin. The mantle curves upward over the side of the shell and secretes onto the surface a smooth, glossy, glowing porcellaneous layer.

The shell is elongate, almost cylindrical, and grows to a height of some 45–50 mm. The ground colour is brown to grey, often with two paler lines. Both ends are coloured orange and are marked with a pair of black spots.

This mollusc is a predatory species found on muddy and sandy bottoms, generally at great depths.

Erronea pyrum LINNÉ

Erronea pyrum has a smooth, pear-shaped shell. The aperture is somewhat wider in the middle. The surface is a glossy, glowing orange to brownish-gold, with darker spots and lines.

This species is also predatory. It is found on muddy and sandy bottoms, often on corals, generally at depths of twenty to fifty metres.

Luria lurida 1
Erronea pyrum 2

1

2

Galeodea echinophora LINNÉ

Cassidae

The shell of this gastropod mollusc is comparatively large and strong, reaching a height of 60 mm and a breadth of 45 mm. It is conical to ovate and has seven inflated whorls, the last of which is massive. The siphonal canal is large and curved backward, and has a deep channel.

The surface is glossy and richly patterned. All the whorls are covered with parallel rows of spiral ridges, the upper edge of each whorl being marked by a row of rugged, spiny tubercles. The ground colour is reddish or brownish-yellow; the lip is porcelain white.

This is a predatory species feeding on other molluscs, worms and crustaceans. Its saliva contains sulphuric acid and aspartic acid which help break up the firm shells of its victims.

Galeodea echinophora is regularly found, but not in large numbers, on muddy and sandy bottoms colonized by corals, *Sycon* sponges and bryozoans, in the deeper parts of oceans.

The decorative shell is sought after by collectors and is used in making ornamental objects. Besides this, *G. echinophora* is an edible species gathered for use as human food, mainly in winter.

Mediterranean Tunshell

Doliidae

Tonna galea LINNÉ

Tonna galea is a true giant among the gastropod molluscs inhabiting the Mediterranean, the shell attaining a diameter of about 250 mm. There are five slightly raised whorls separated by a deep suture. The final whorl is greatly inflated and the aperture is broadly ovate. The shell is light, thin and transparent and marked with conspicuous spiral grooves and ribs that are alternately broad and narrow. When empty it is almost white, but when inhabited by the animal it is coloured brown.

A remarkable ability which nature has bestowed upon this animal was discovered quite by chance when it was observed to eject a stream of saliva on to marble which suddenly began to hiss and foam. Chemical analysis has shown that the saliva contains three to four percent of sulphuric acid. *T. galea* is a merciless predator that attacks sea-urchins, starfish, sea-cucumbers and large bivalves. Its saliva paralyzes the body of its prey and at the same time corrodes and breaks up its protective shell. With its long proboscis it then eats the soft fleshy parts, and in the case of smaller prey, devours its victim whole.

T. galea inhabits the Mediterranean, generally living at great depths on seabeds composed of mud or muddy sand.

Rapana thomasiana Crosse Thaididae

(syn. *R. bezoar* L.)

This large predatory gastropod mollusc was introduced into the European seas from the Far East. The shell is large and thick and consists of seven to eight whorls separated by a deep suture. It reaches a height of 190 mm and a breadth of 160 mm. The siphonal canal is comparatively short and wide, the channel deep and open. The shell surface is marked with a distinct pattern of numerous parallel spiral ribs crossed by deep transverse growth grooves. The upper edge of each whorl is covered with rugged tubercles. The colour ranges from pale yellow to reddish-brown, often with a darker pattern of spiral and radiating lines. The inside of the aperture is bright orange-red, yellow or brown.

This species is native to the southern parts of the Sea of Japan. In the nineteen-forties it was introduced into the Black Sea and thence spread very rapidly. Today it is very plentiful especially on the northern, western and eastern shores. It has also been found in the Sea of Azov.

R. thomasiana lives on sandy bottoms and on rocks from the shoreline down to depths of about thirty metres. It is a predatory mollusc, feeding chiefly on mussels. The decorative shell is a popular souvenir with visitors to the Black Sea coast.

The shell of this species is oval to ovate and is composed of six to seven whorls covered with cone-shaped, radial tubercles. The siphonal canal is narrow and very long. The height of the shell may be as much as 90 mm. The surface is furrowed by a great number of parallel spiral ridges crossed by radiating growth lines. The ground colour is yellowish-white, the aperture orange-yellow.

Bolinus brandaris inhabits sandy and gravelly bottoms and is also found on seaweed at depths of more than fifteen to twenty metres. A predator, it feeds mainly on bivalves.

This gastropod mollusc, plain and uninteresting at first glance, was of great commercial value for thousands of years for the almost colourless fluid secreted by a special gland in the mantle cavity which was used to make a dye. When exposed to sunlight the fluid changes colour, turning yellow, then green, and last of all purple to rich magenta. This was the famous Tyrian purple known to the ancients. Because of its fastness it was used for centuries to dye the costly garments of high lay and church dignitaries. In the days of the Roman Empire and even later it was worth its weight in gold and purple robes were a mark of wealth and power. Of interest, however, is the fact that to this day we do not know what function the fluid fulfils for the mollusc itself.

Truncularìopsis trunculus Linné Muricidae

The shell of this species, growing to a height of 65 mm, is oval and is composed of six to seven whorls. The surface is marked with a great number of fine spiral ribs crossed by transverse grooves bearing tubercles and spines formed during growth. The mouth of the shell has a toothed outer and smooth inner margin. The siphonal canal is fairly long and slightly curved backward. The coloration of the shell is generally grey-white to pale brown with three dark violet bands shining through on the inside of the mouth.

It lives on stones and rocks among growths of sea grasses and seaweed in the upper regions of the littoral zone.

Truncularìopsis trunculus, like *Bolinus brandaris*, has a special gland secreting a fluid which was once used to make the costly dye known as Tyrian purple. Records of its extensive production in ancient Rome have been preserved to this day. The hill outside the Italian city of Taranto called 'monte testaceo' (shell hill) by the local people is composed entirely of the shells of these molluscs.

These bivalves are still of great commercial value today, and are used as food in Italy and other Mediterranean countries where they are known as 'sconciglio', 'bullo maschio' and 'garusolo maschio'.

Sting Winkle

Muricidae

Ocenebra erinacea LINNÉ

Ocenebra erinacea has a conical shell up to 60 mm high, composed of four to seven whorls. The aperture terminates in a closed siphonal canal. The surface is richly sculptured and articulated and covered with spines. Besides the main spines there are smaller auxiliary spines on certain spiral ridges.

The colour is extremely variable, ranging from yellowish-white to dark brown. Some ridges are furthermore marked with darker stripes.

O. erinacea is common on all types of hard sea bottoms and also on jetties, preferring shallower depths. It is a predator just like other related species of this family. Its chief victims are bivalves, which it forces open by the pressure of its foot, thereupon inserting its proboscis and eating the soft fleshy parts. Members of the family Muricidae also attack other hard-shelled animals such as crabs, feeding on the fleshy parts by inserting the proboscis through the anal opening.

O. erinacea is an edible species and is also collected for its shells which are employed in making various ornamental objects.

Columbella rustica Linné — Columbellidae

This species is a medium-sized prosobranch gastropod with a pointed, ovate shell attaining a height of nearly 20 mm. The whorls are placed so close together that they appear to merge, the suture being only faintly discernible. There are eight to nine whorls, the last one larger than the whole of the remaining spire. The mouth of the shell is narrowed practically to a slit with a thickened and toothed outer lip. When the animal is alive the aperture is closed by an elliptic operculum. The siphonal canal is broad and fairly long with a deep channel and faint notch at the end.

The surface of the shell is smooth without any marked sculpture. The coloration exhibits great variation. The ground colour is white to yellow and when the outermost layer that covers the shell (the periostracum) is rubbed off one can see the attractive reddish to black pattern consisting of irregular, interrupted, wavy bands and spots. The top whorls are tinted violet. The mouth of the shell is white, the teeth a darker colour.

C. rustica is generally distributed and occurs in great numbers, chiefly in the uppermost region of the rocky littoral zone just below the surface of the sea. The attractive shells are often cast up on the shore.

Common Whelk

Buccinidae

Buccinum undatum LINNÉ

The shell of *Buccinum undatum* is ovate to conical with six to eight inflated, highly raised whorls separated by a deep suture. It attains a height of 110 mm and a width of 65 mm. The surface is marked with a distinct pattern composed of numerous spiral ribs crossed regularly by longitudinal wrinkles. The ground colour is greyish-yellow, the thin organic outer layer is dark brown. The mouth is yellowish-white. The shape, size, as well as coloration of the shell, exhibit marked variations. Individuals inhabiting the intertidal zone have a thick, large and heavy shell; those that dwell in calmer waters at greater depths have a thin shell of greater height.

B. undatum is widely distributed on stony and sandy bottoms from the shoreline down to depths of about one hundred and fifty to two hundred metres. It is a carnivorous species feeding chiefly on dead animals, the sharp teeth of the radula tearing out scraps of flesh about the size of hazelnuts.

The eggs are laid in bean-sized capsules stuck together in clumps. The young do not abandon the capsules during growth, feeding at this time on eggs of their own species. Though this means that there are fewer offspring, they are more developed when finally freed from the capsule.

In many areas *B. undatum* is gathered as human food. Fishermen often use it as bait.

Euthria cornea LINNÉ — Buccinidae

The shell of *Euthria cornea* is a strong, narrow cone up to 50 mm high. A characteristic feature of this species is that the whorls grow closely to one another and are not separated by a deep suture. The surface is almost smooth or only very finely patterned with spiral grooves. More distinct are the radiating growth lines. The mouth of the shell is oval with a slightly thickened, finely toothed lip. The siphonal canal is wide, of medium length, curved backward and notched at the end.

The colour is variable. In older individuals the grey to brown ground colour is predominant, the surface pattern consisting only of a network of paler spiral and radiating lines and spots. The smaller shells of younger individuals have a more distinctive pattern, most pronounced being the row of spiral lines composed of alternating white and dark brown streaks and spots.

E. cornea is a carnivorous species that eats both dead animals as well as various live molluscs, crustaceans and worms. It occurs on sandy and hard bottoms as well as on stony ground, generally at greater depths. It is widely distributed in the Mediterranean and Atlantic.

Dog Whelk

Buccinidae

Nucella lapillus Linné

The shell of *Nucella lapillus* is ovate with a pointed apex and is composed of five to six inflated whorls separated by a fairly deep suture. It is thick and firm and closed by an operculum. It reaches a height of 35–45 mm. The aperture is oval, the lips are thickened and the outer margin is often toothed.

The surface of the shell is marked with spiral ribs; the older whorls usually have three ribs each, the final whorl a further eight to ten smaller ribs.

The colour is extremely variable and is influenced by the animal's diet. It is generally whitish-yellow to greenish, sometimes marked with brown spiral lines. The aperture is white or bluish to pinkish-brown.

N. lapillus is a carnivorous species that feeds chiefly on bivalves and cirripeds. With its radula it bores a small hole in their hard shells through which it inserts its proboscis and eats the victim's flesh. Moving prey is held fast by the foot. Its predatory habits often make *N. lapillus* an unpleasant pest because it causes great damage to commercially valuable species such as the popular edible cockle *Cerastoderma edule.*

N. lapillus is widely distributed on the European coast of the Atlantic and is one of the commonest molluscs of British waters. It inhabits sandy and stony ground in the littoral zone.

Cantharus d'orbignyi PAYRAUDEAU — Buccinidae

This species is one of the smaller members of the order Prosobranchia, its elongate shell reaching a height of 20–25 mm. The inflated whorls are marked with a pronounced pattern formed by regular raised longitudinal ridges crossed by well-defined spiral grooves. The individual coils are separated by a deep suture. The mouth of the shell is oval and thickened and has a row of strong teeth on the inner margin.

The coloration is extremely variable. The ground colour is usually light brown to brownish-black with a white spiral line. The mouth of the shell is white to violet.

Cantharus d'orbignyi is just as predacious as *Buccinum undatum*, its victims, however, being proportionately smaller animals. It makes its home among the vegetation of the littoral zone, being commonly found near the seaweed *Ulva*. It is often found in large numbers in harbours and other places with greatly polluted water.

The interesting and distinctively patterned shells with variable coloration are eagerly sought after by collectors and can usually be found in any collection of seashells.

Pisania maculosa LAMARCK Buccinidae

This species, though a medium-sized prosobranch, is one of the smaller members of the family. The compact shell has a fairly high cone-shaped spiral composed of six to seven whorls, the last one being relatively large. The mouth of the shell is longish, elliptic and toothed inside, with a long raised rib running from each tooth into the interior of the shell. There is a single large tooth at the base. The siphonal canal is short and broad, as is the channel. The shell surface is marked by a dense network of spiral furrows, six to seven on each of the upper whorls and a great many on the last one.

The shell's attractiveness is enhanced by the variable coloration. The ground colour is brownish-green to coffee-brown with white spots and streaks of various sizes either scattered irregularly over the surface or else arranged in interrupted spiral lines, which are most numerous on the final whorl. The mouth of the shell is violet with a white central band and white teeth and ribs.

Pisania maculosa lives among the vegetation of the rocky littoral zone, chiefly among growths of the seaweed *Ulva*. It is particularly common in the polluted waters of coastal hamlets and harbours.

Knobbed Triton

Tritoniidae

Charonia lampas LAMARCK

This is one of the most rugged gastropod molluscs of the European seas. The tall, conical, very thick shell has eight to nine whorls and measures up to 30 cm in height. The surface is sculptured with a large number of broad and narrow spiral ribs and blunt knobs crossed by deep radial grooves marking the growth lines. The colour may be white, yellow to pale brown with brown radial stripes and marbling.

Charonia lampas was known in ancient Rome, where it was used as a war trumpet called the 'buccina'. To this day it is employed by Italian fishermen as a means of signalling at sea. This species is carnivorous. Unlike most other predatory gastropods, however, it does not tear the flesh of its victim but swallows it whole. It feeds on molluscs, starfish and various crustaceans as well as fish, and is one of the fiercest predators of the seabed. Its saliva contains aspartic acid which helps break up the firm calcareous shells of its victims.

C. lampas has a remarkable method of protecting itself. When disturbed it suddenly thrusts its shell forward and strikes it against the seabed, thereby frightening off even a large predator.

Netted Dog Whelk

Nassidae

Nassarius reticulatus LINNÉ

The shell of this species is firm, conical to ovate, and composed of eight to nine whorls separated by a very shallow suture. It grows to a length of 32 mm and a breadth of 18 mm. The surface is conspicuously marked by a large number of broad, flat ribs that form a spiral pattern. The colour is very variable, ranging from pale yellow to dark brown. Pale shells are patterned with dark brown stripes.

Nassarius reticulatus is a carnivorous species and an important member of the sea's 'sanitation force', feeding chiefly on the flesh of various dead animals such as worms, molluscs, cephalopods and fish. With its radula it rasps out pieces of the animal's flesh.

It lives buried in sand, leaving its hideout, however, as soon as it scents prey. These gastropod molluscs will converge on a piece of flesh from as far away as twenty to thirty metres. Their greatest enemy is the starfish. When they wish to put a safe distance between themselves and a predator they do so by a reflex action consisting of eight to nine violent leaps in succession.

N. reticulatus is widely distributed and plentiful along the coast of Europe from Norway to the Mediterranean and as far as the Black Sea.

Cyclope neritea Linné — Nassidae

The shell of *Cyclope neritea* differs sharply in shape from those of its relatives. It is very flat, thick and button-like, composed of four to five flat whorls connecting closely with one another. The last whorl is very large and makes up the greater part of the shell. The mouth is oval with a thickened outer lip. The siphonal canal is very short and is marked by a deep dorsal notch. The shell reaches a height of 8 mm and a width of 16 mm.

The surface is smooth and glossy, brightly coloured and variable. The ground colour is usually pale yellow to reddish-brown, and covered with an extremely variable network pattern on the upper side. The flat underside is usually a light colour without the network pattern. The mouth is yellowish. The inside of the shell is ornamented with the same rufous-red network pattern as the outside. The unusual shape and delicate variable coloration make it a very attractive shell.

C. neritea lives on sandy bottoms, usually at shallow depths, though it sometimes descends to depths of forty to fifty metres. It is very plentiful and has a widespread geographic distribution extending from the Atlantic on the south-western coast of Europe through the Mediterranean and on to the Black Sea.

This is one of the smaller species of prosobranchs. The slender, spindle-shaped shell is composed of seven whorls, the last of which is slightly higher than all the others combined. It grows to a height of about 20 mm. The mouth of the shell is comparatively narrow and elongated and is terminated by a broad siphonal canal. The external margin of the aperture is marked with spiral furrows; the inside margin bears three raised folds.

The shell surface is smooth and marked with slightly raised longitudinal ridges (especially on the final whorl), which are discernible with the naked eye.

The colour of the shell, as the specific name indicates, is ebony-brown. There is, however, a marked variation in the richness of this colour. The shell is furthermore ornamented with a single light brown to white spiral band. The mouth of the shell is also brown, except for the white folds on the inner margin.

Mitra ebenus is generally distributed in the rocky littoral zone and is also found on firm sandy seabeds in the Mediterranean, particularly among the seaweed that forms a covering on rocks, and also among the grass of submarine meadows.

Mediterranean Cone Shell

Conidae

Conus ventricosus GMELIN

The shells of these gastropod molluscs have one peculiarity – the inner partitions between the individual whorls gradually disappear during the process of growth and the inside of the shell thus becomes a simple cavity. The aperture is long and narrow and closed by an operculum. The shell reaches a height of 20–30 mm. The surface is almost entirely smooth except for a series of radiating lines marking the growth zones. The ground colour is grey-green to reddish with reddish-brown or brownish-yellow streaks and irregular spots.

This species has a poison gland which discharges a fluid that paralyzes its prey. The poison is injected into the body of its victim by means of the radula, which is supplied with cone-shaped teeth resembling hollow needles. Cone shells are predatory and feed on bristle worms, various crustaceans and molluscs. Large tropical species of the genus *Conus* may even sting humans and cause painful wounds, occasionally fatal. The comparatively small European species is harmless in this respect.

Conus ventricosus lives in large numbers in the stony littoral waters of the Mediterranean, chiefly among seaweed.

In some places cone shells are collected for food. Most highly valued, however, are their shells, especially those of the tropical species, for which collectors often pay fantastic sums of money.

Canoe Shell

Scaphandridae

Scaphander lignarius LINNÉ

This species is the only representative of the subclass Opisthobranchia (sea-slugs) in this book. The shell, very different from the usual type, is disproportionately small, so that it affords no shelter for the animal in times of need. The spiral is completely covered by the greatly expanded final whorl. The aperture is the same height as the shell, being broad at the bottom. *Scaphander lignarius* may grow to a height of 70 mm.

The surface sculpturing is composed of numerous parallel spiral grooves so regular that they give the impression of having been cut by a diamond guided by the hand of an expert glass cutter. The colour is brownish-red with dark bands. The mouth is bluish-white.

S. lignarius is found on soft sediments and on sand. It feeds chiefly on scaphopods which live buried in sand. When moving through the sand the animal's expanded foot and head-shield, formed by the united tentacles, function like a snowplough. Its victim, a scaphopod or other mollusc buried in the sand, is swallowed whole including the shell, which is crushed in the gizzard by three calcareous plates. With its great appetite, however, *Scaphander* will eat any kind of animal food from minute foraminiferans to polychaete worms.

Common Tusk Shell

Dentaliidae

Dentalium dentale LINNÉ

Dentalium dentale has a large, 30—50 mm long, slightly curved shell resembling a small elephant tusk. The surface is marked by eighteen to twenty longitudinal grooves. The colour is generally white, sometimes with reddish bands.

On each side of the head is a tuft of long filaments with club-shaped ends, serving as tactile organs and used also for capturing food. The radula is capable of crushing the shells of small molluscs, crustaceans, foraminiferans and the like.

This species lives on muddy or sandy bottoms, sometimes also in fine gravel, buried in the ground with only the end projecting. It is a fairly active animal that ploughs through the mud and sand of the seabed.

It is found from the shoreline to depths of several hundred metres.

Dentalium vulgare DA COSTA

Dentalium vulgare has a narrower shell, about 60 mm long. The surface is marked with very fine longitudinal grooves and is a mat milky white.

The body structure, way of life and method of capturing and digesting food is the same as in *D. dentale*.

D. vulgare, however, has a more limited vertical distribution, generally inhabiting waters closer to the shore, mostly at depths of about thirty to seventy metres.

Dentalium dentale 1
Dentalium vulgare 2

2
1

Noah's Ark Shell

Arcidae

Arca noae LINNÉ

The shell of *Arca noae* is longish, boat-shaped and sloping at the rear, this being the reason for the name given to this mollusc. It grows to a length of 70 mm, a height of 35 mm and a thickness of 36 mm. The beaks of the valves are very prominent and wide apart. The margin of the hinge is long and straight and covered with numerous teeth. The surface is covered with radiating ridges crossed at right angles by the growth lines. The outer surface is coloured pale grey to brown with darker transverse, often zig-zag, reddish bands. The interior is coloured dark brown.

A. noae occurs in large numbers on all kinds of stony, gravelly and sandy bottoms and at all depths, often on the empty shells of mussels and other bivalves. The foot is very broad and has a flat base, similar to that of gastropods, thus enabling the animal to move fairly rapidly even over the smooth surface of stones and shells. Adult individuals generally inhabit the upper regions of the littoral zone firmly anchored among seaweed.

This species is widely distributed along the Atlantic coast of Europe and Africa as far as Senegal. It is also found throughout the whole of the Mediterranean. It is an edible species which is eaten raw.

Dog Cockle

Glycymeridae

Glycymeris glycymeris LINNÉ

This species has a large, strong, nearly circular shell terminating rather abruptly at the hind end. It may grow to as much as 80 mm in diameter. The margin is flattened and expanded. The upper shell bears a greater number of transverse grooves of more or less identical size. The periostracum is velvety and coloured brown and where it has been rubbed off the dirty white ground colour shines through. Fine grooves radiate from the beaks to the margins; these are crossed by strong concentric lines and growth bands. In young individuals the whitish ground colour is spotted brown. In older individuals these markings may even be irregular zig-zag bands. The lower margin of the valve is crenulated inside. This mollusc lives buried in sand or muddy sand.

The strong and durable shells far outlast the animals that inhabit them. In many places they may be found in great quantities on the shore at the low water mark and they also form an important part of muddy and gravelly regions of the seabed at depths of twenty to fifty metres. *Glycymeris glycymeris* is plentiful in the Mediterranean and on the European shores of the Atlantic.

Common Mussel or **European Edible Mussel**

Mytilidae

Mytilus galloprovincialis LAMARCK

The shell of *Mytilus galloprovincialis* is wedge-shaped, attaining a length of 60–80 mm, a height of 40 mm and a thickness of 35 mm. Both shape and size exhibit marked variations, being influenced by the quantity of food, amount of living space, and the salinity and temperature of the water and water currents. The surface is almost smooth, marked only by the growth lines.

The colour is blue-black to yellow-brown, often with darker radiating lines. The inside of the shell is bluish-white. The animal is yellow and has a strong, tongue-shaped foot coloured brownish-violet.

This mussel lives firmly attached to rocks and other solid objects by the aid of its byssal threads. In suitable places, i.e. on stones just below the surface strongly pounded by waves, these mussels may be found growing in extensive beds. At ebb tide they tolerate short periods out of water. They feed on strained plankton and organic debris brought by the currents.

M. galloprovincialis is an important species for the fishing industry. It is widely consumed as food and has been cultivated in mussel beds since ancient times. It is native to the Mediterranean and the Black Sea, but ranges as far north as south-west England.

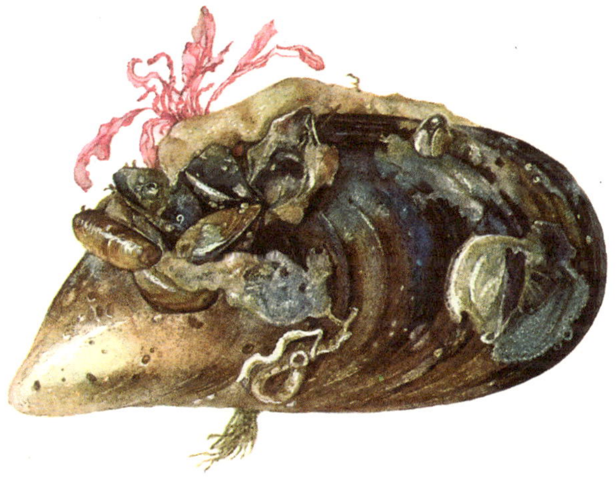

Bearded Horse Mussel

Mytilidae

Modiolus barbatus LINNÉ

One glance at the shape of the shell gives a clear indication that the genus *Modiolus* is closely related to the genus *Mytilus*.

The shell of *Modiolus barbatus* is irregular, bean-shaped and relatively thin. It reaches up to 60 mm in length, 30 mm in height and 25 mm in thickness. The anterior end is short and rounded, the posterior end with the lunule is prominently raised. The apex is blunt and located at the front. The periostracum is thick and felt-like at the front, the hind sections of the valves are shaggy with a fringe of bearded thorns extending beyond the shell margin, hence the specific name *barbatus*.

The shell surface, especially in older individuals, is wrinkled and marked with distinct concentric growth lines. The colour is dark brown on the outside and grey to bluish on the inside.

M. barbatus also spins byssal threads with which it attaches itself to the substratum. It is commonly found in great numbers on rocky, gravelly and sandy bottoms of the littoral zone, frequently attaching itself to the shells of other bivalves, clumps of corals and bryozoans. It shows a marked preference for living in rock crevices and between stones. It feeds on minute marine plankton.

M. barbatus is widespread on the shores of the Atlantic.

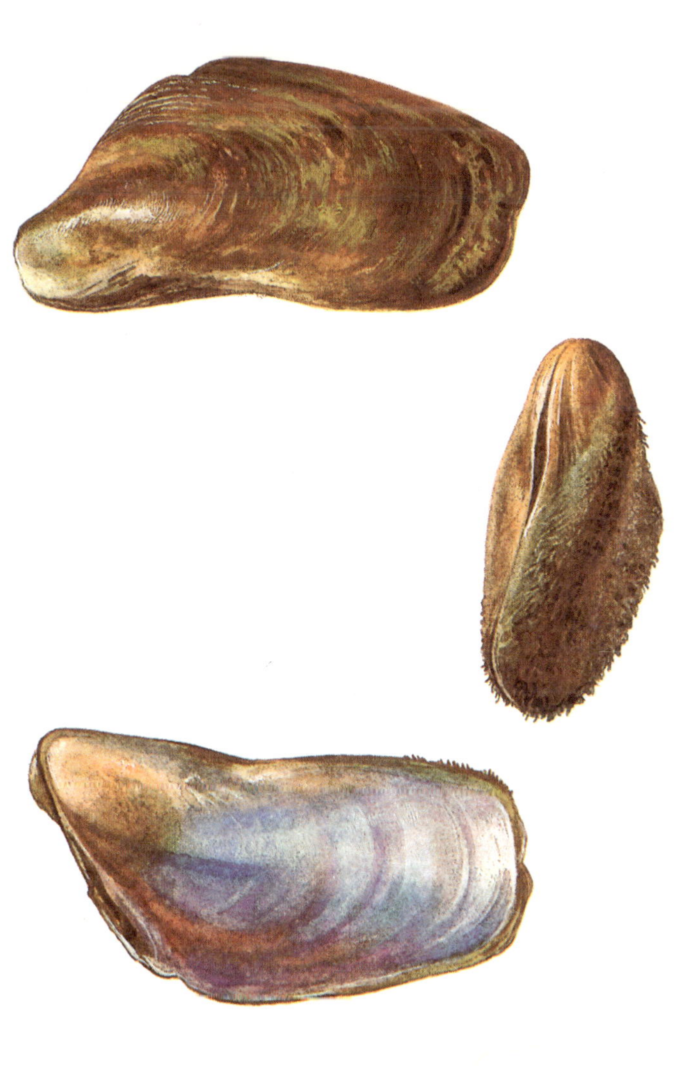

Marbled Crenella

Mytilidae

Musculus marmoratus FORBES

This relatively small species has a paper-thin, transparent shell, ovate in shape. The beaks of the valves, located near the anterior edge, look distinctly inflated because the anterior section, i.e. the lunule, is greatly shortened. The lower margin is practically straight. The shell reaches up to 15 mm in length, 9 mm in height and 8 mm in thickness.

The surface is divided into three sections and has an interesting pattern. The forward end is marked with fifteen to twenty radiating ribs, the posterior end with twenty-five to thirty-five radiating ribs and the centre of the valves is plain.

The ground colour is yellow-green to white with red marbling. The inside is pearly opalescent.

Musculus marmoratus lives on muddy and sandy bottoms of the littoral and adjacent deeper zones, attaching itself to the substratum with its byssus, particularly to ascidians (sea squirts). It has a scattered distribution.

M. marmoratus is very widespread. Its range extends from the European coast of the Atlantic northward as far as Norway. It is also found throughout the whole of the Mediterranean, making its way via the Bosporus to parts of the Black Sea.

Noble Pen Shell

Pinnidae

Pinna nobilis LINNÉ

Pinna nobilis may rightfully be called the queen of European sea-shells. Its shell, shaped like a cudgel, grows to a length of 80 – 90 cm. The outside is covered with thick, convex scales, which in young individuals cloak the greater part of the shell surface, and is coloured reddish-brown to greenish-brown. The inside walls are rufous-red with a pearly gloss.

This species lives with its front, pointed end embedded in sand. Besides this it is anchored to the bottom by the aid of long and very tough byssal threads. In Italy these threads ('shell silk') are spun and worked into gloves and various other articles.

P. nobilis is remarkable also for its symbiotic association with the small (only 15 mm long) crab *Pinnotheres veterum*. As soon as the valves open one can see this small lodger in the slit. If safe to do so, the crab climbs out of its shelter and forages for food in the close vicinity of its host. When danger threatens it quickly darts back inside and the shell instantly closes, a reflex action caused by mechanical irritation of the host's mantle. This lovely shell is found in great numbers both in the Atlantic and the Mediterranean and is considered to be a great delicacy.

Jacob's Scallop or **Pilgrim's Scallop** Pectinidae

Pecten jacobaeus LINNÉ

This species is one of the largest and most beautiful of European bivalves. The shell reaches up to 130 mm in length, 120 mm in height and 30 mm in thickness. The valves exhibit marked inequality of shape, the right one being very convex, and taking the form of a cup, the left flat, forming a lid to the cup. The surface is ornamented with fifteen to sixteen radiating, longitudinally grooved ribs. The furrows between the ribs and the ears on either side of the beak are likewise grooved.

The beauty of the shell is enhanced by the ornamental patterning of the surface and the variable coloration. The right, convex valve is usually white to pale pink, the other valve rufous to reddish, patterned with brown to violet concentric lines, bands and spots. The shells of this species have been used since ancient times as cups and bowls and have been adopted as company trademarks, club emblems, etc.

P. jacobaeus lives unattached on sandy and coralline bottoms. It is remarkable in that, like few other bivalves, it is capable of swimming through water by rapidly clapping its valves.

This species is widely distributed chiefly in the Mediterranean. In Italy it is considered a gastronomic delicacy, having been valued far higher than oysters since ancient times.

Queen Scallop

Pectinidae

Aequipecten opercularis **LINNÉ**

The shell of this species is nearly circular in shape and very firm. It grows to about 80 mm in length, 75 mm in height and 24 mm in thickness. This scallop also has two asymmetrical valves with unequal ears. The right valve is somewhat flatter and the left one more convex. The surface is marked by eighteen to twenty-two radiating ribs and the intervening spaces bear wavy grooves. The widely variable coloration enhances the attractiveness of this scallop, orange, yellow, white and red and white mottled shells all being found. Sometimes one may even find a small pearl inside the shell of a live individual.

Aequipecten opercularis occurs on various types of bottoms but is more common on sandy ground. Like *Pecten jacobaeus* it is capable of swimming; when swimming it greatly resembles a flitting, brightly coloured submarine butterfly. In the Atlantic its distribution extends from the Canary Islands to the Lofoten; it is also common in the Mediterranean.

It is a very popular edible species much in demand on the market and therefore intensively harvested by coastline fishermen.

Variegated Scallop

Pectinidae

Chlamys varia LINNÉ

The shell of this species is conspicuously raised. It reaches a length of 50 mm, a height of 60 mm and a thickness of 18 mm. The ears are unequal and differ in shape.

The surface of the shell is prominently sculptured with twenty-six to thirty radiating ribs bearing raised, thorn-like plates at regular intervals. Adjacent plates form regular concentric rows.

The bright and variable coloration of this lovely scallop makes it even more attractive. It is generally yellow-white, red, brown or black, with a pronounced pattern that also shows variation, hence its scientific name as well as certain common names.

Chlamys varia inhabits all types of bottom, preferably sandy ground and often firm coralline ground, being more common at greater depths. It is a very widespread species on the European coast of the Atlantic, extending northward as far as the western shores of Norway. It is also very abundant throughout the whole of the Mediterranean.

It is an edible mollusc of great commercial value and therefore very widely gathered by coastline fishermen.

Flexopecten flexuosus Poli

Pectinidae

Like other scallops, *Flexopecten flexuosus* has an asymmetrical shell, the right valve being somewhat more inflated than the left one. The ears at each side of the beak are almost of equal size. The circular shell grows to a height of 45 mm and a thickness of 17 mm.

The surface is ornamented with five to six broad, rounded, radiating ribs. The spaces in between are much broader than the ribs themselves and often bear further auxiliary ribs that are always narrower and lower than the main ones.

The ground colour is whitish to grey with an irregular and extremely variable pattern of brownish-red spots and lines and white opalescent spots.

F. flexuosus is widely distributed throughout the Mediterranean. It is very common and occurs in large numbers on all types of bottoms, chiefly on sandy and muddy substrata.

It is an edible species of great commercial value and therefore gathered in large numbers. The ornamental shells are often used in making various small articles and souvenirs.

Flexopecten glaber Linné　　Pectinidae

This medium-sized scallop also has an asymmetrical shell, the left valve being somewhat more inflated than the right one. The ears are nearly the same size. The round shell is as long as it is high (up to 55 mm), and up to 13 mm thick.

The surface is marked by ten to eleven radiating ribs of almost equal thickness with equally broad hollows in between. The inside of the shell is also ribbed.

The shell is very brightly coloured, the ground colour usually being vermilion to orange with paler lines and spots.

Flexopecten glaber is a common species of the Mediterranean, and has also made its way to the Black Sea. It occurs in large numbers on various types of seabed, descending to depths of fifty to sixty metres, but is partial to sandy ground.

File Shell

Limidae

Lima lima LINNÉ

At first glance it is evident that these bivalves are closely related to the scallops (family Pectinidae). The shell is large, firm ana only slightly rounded, but markedly raised with prominent ears at each side of the beak. It reaches a length of 35 mm, a height of 50 mm and a thickness of 18 mm. It is very ornamental but is neither conspicuously coloured nor patterned, its delicate beauty resting in its porcellaneous whiteness and pronounced sculpturing. The entire surface is ornamented with nine to twenty-four prominent ribs radiating from the apex to the margin. The furrows between the ribs are smooth and deep. The ribs themselves are ornamented with regular rows of projecting scales arranged in concentric lines that are coincidental with the growth lines of the shell. Corrugation corresponding to the radiating ribs and concentric growth bands is discernible also on the glossy, porcelain-like interior of the shell.

Lima lima is a common species of the littoral zone of the Mediterranean and of the coasts of south-western Europe. It lives in large numbers on hard, stony bottoms among corals and sea sponges.

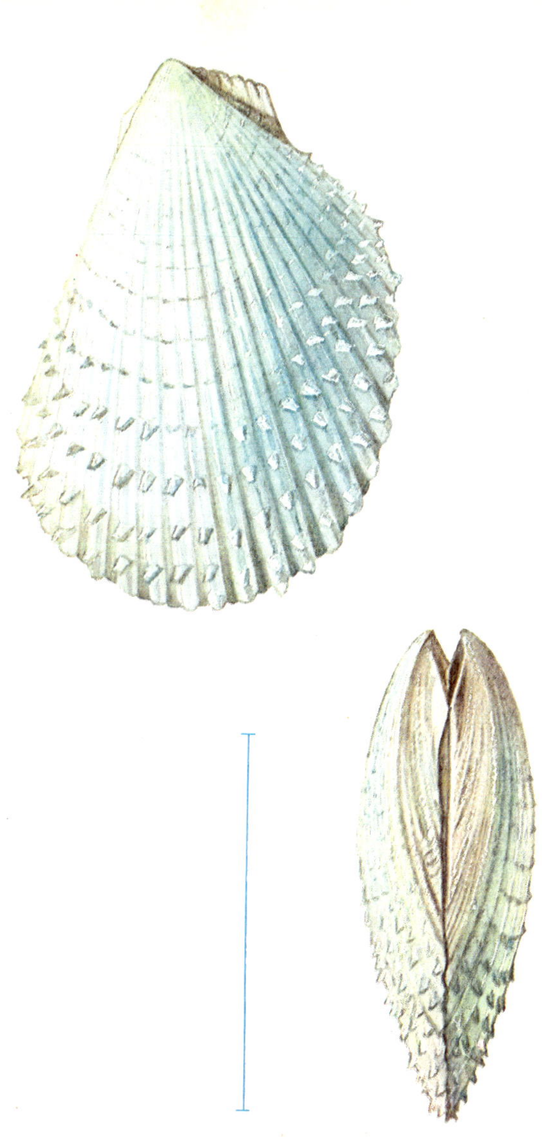

Swollen File Shell

Limidae

Mantellum inflatum CHEMNITZ

The shell of *Mantellum inflatum* is large, thin and very high, growing up to 28 mm in length, 40 mm in height and 24 mm in thickness. The narrow apex is prominent and projects beyond the upper edge. Both valves are greatly inflated.

The surface of the fragile shell is ornamented with a rich pattern consisting of about thirty-five slightly raised radiating ribs with fine grooves in between. The radiating sculpture is crossed at irregular intervals by concentric growth lines.

The coloration is very simple, generally white or pale rufous.

M. inflatum is widespread throughout the Mediterranean, and has also made its way through the Sea of Marmara and the Bosporus as far as the southern regions of the Black Sea. It occurs commonly and in great numbers on various types of bottoms, though it favours sandy and muddy ground. Frequently, however, it is also found among corals, sponges and other marine growths. It is capable of flitting through the water like certain species of scallops.

Common Oyster or **European Edible Oyster**

Ostreidae

Ostrea edulis LINNÉ

The shells of oysters show marked variation in shape, thickness and coloration, all three factors being influenced by the conditions of the environment. The lower valve is convex, cup-shaped, and firmly cemented to the substratum, the upper valve is flat and functions as a lid. The shells generally attain a diameter of 70 – 100 mm or more. Most oysters live to an age of some ten to twelve years; large individuals, 150 mm across or even larger, are often more than thirty years old.

The oyster is a very common mollusc of the European coast of the Atlantic, its distribution extending from Norway to as far as North Africa. It requires water with a fairly high salinity and therefore is not found in the Baltic Sea. It prefers the shallow waters of the shoreline with a firm stony bottom. The western coast of Europe was at one time fringed with an almost continuous belt of oyster banks from Denmark all the way to northern Spain. The intensive and unregulated harvesting of the oysters, however, almost entirely destroyed this rich and lucrative supply, reckless dredging with iron nets being chiefly responsible for the devastation. Nowadays this method of gathering oysters has been limited and the beds are being gradually restored.

Oysters thrive best near river estuaries rich in microscopic organic debris and plankton, which they strain from the water. *Ostrea edulis* is a very common species highly valued as food.

Ostrea edulis adriatica LAMARCK — Ostreidae

Ostrea edulis is an extremely variable species comprising many members of diverse shape, determined largely by their surroundings, which were often described as a separate species. One such variety considered by some authors as a separate, distinct species is the one shown in the illustration. The shell of *O.e. adriatica* is thick, sloping and ovate. The upper valve is covered with raised lamellae and a great number of folds.

The oyster has been harvested for food for thousands of years. It was gathered in large quantities by Paleolithic Man as testified to by the great number of shells in the refuse holes of his settlements. Oysters have also been cultivated for centuries, since the days of ancient Rome. Nowadays they are widely cultivated mainly in England, France and the United States. Culture beds in England are very extensive and cover areas of up to twenty-seven square miles. A great number of local varieties are known to lovers of this delicacy, some more highly prized than others.

Oysters have many natural enemies that not only destroy them in their natural habitats but often also become dangerous pests of culture beds. These include numerous predatory gastropods, crabs, starfish, and, in the early stage of the oyster's development, also fish. Further dangerous pests of culture beds are mussels, which compete with the oysters for food.

Hoof Shell

Chamidae

Chama gryphoides LINNÉ

This bivalve has a strong shell of medium size, about 20 mm across and about as long as it is wide.

Its sessile way of life has resulted in great changes in the structure of the shell in the same way as in oysters. The two halves are asymmetrical. The left (lower) valve, which is cemented to the substratum, is larger and forms a cup, the right (upper) one is smaller and forms a lid to the cup. The general appearance is very bizarre. The concentric growth bands, running irregularly over the surface, are covered with thorn-like processes. The surface is whitish, the inside of the valves brownish-violet.

Since it lives firmly cemented to the substratum this mollusc is dependent on a regular supply of small food particles, such as organic debris and microscopic plankton, which it strains from the water.

Chama gryphoides is plentiful mostly on rocky shores at shallow depths where the water is warmed by the sun and also affords an abundance of suitable food.

Common Cockle or **European Edible Cockle**

Cardiidae

Cerastoderma edule LINNÉ

Cerastoderma edule is one of the commonest of European cockles. It grows to a length of up to 50 mm. The shell is distinctively sculptured and bears twenty to twenty-eight, flatly rounded ribs. The ground colour is white to yellowish, the posterior half often dark and patterned with darker concentric circles.

This species is extraordinarily adaptable and is very tolerant of variations in the salinity of water. It is very variable in shape as well as size, being smaller in brackish waters. It is plentiful in all European seas.

Common in muddy and sandy locations, it occurs in large numbers in the shallow waters of lagoons and estuaries whenever there is an abundant supply of organic food. (The most common species found in lagoons is the allied *C. glaucum* Poiret.) It is found in mud, into which it burrows very rapidly by means of jerky movements of its foot. It feeds chiefly on plankton and organic debris filtered from the water.

This cockle is harvested in vast numbers and in some coastal regions forms the staple diet. In the north of Italy it is widely eaten and is known as 'capa tonda'. The shells are used for various purposes, in some places, for instance, for the extraction of lime.

Spiny Cockle

Cardiidae

Acanthocardia aculeata LINNÉ

This is an interesting cockle with a large, fairly thin, heart-shaped shell, which grows to a length of about 80 mm, a height of 75 mm and a thickness of 50 mm. Both valves are markedly convex.

The shell is very ornamental. The prominent radiating ribs (of which there are twenty to twenty-two) are furrowed lengthwise on top, and these furrows are beset with stout curved spines. In older shells these spines are generally broken off, only the strongest and youngest remaining. The ribs as well as the broad flat furrows between them are crossed by fine transverse growth lines.

The coloration consists of delicate pastel hues. The ground colour is usually yellow-brown to reddish with a more pronounced pattern of similarly coloured spiral bands of varying width.

Acanthocardia aculeata is a common species of cockle found in large numbers on soft muddy bottoms of the littoral and sub-littoral zones. An edible species, it is widely gathered both on the European coast of the Atlantic and in the Mediterranean. The shells are often used to make various ornamental objects.

Rough Cockle

Cardiidae

Acanthocardia tuberculata LINNÉ

This cockle has a large, solid, oval shell that is both high and very convex. The length and height of the shell may be as much as 65 mm and the thickness as much as 50 mm.

The surface is distinctively sculptured. Radiating from the beak on each side of the shell are some nineteen to twenty-three rounded ribs, slightly knobbed at intervals. The furrows between the ribs are patterned with fine transverse grooves.

The colour of the shell is extremely variable. The ground colour is usually white to rufous, patterned with a number of dark brown to reddish-brown concentric rings that are narrower and closer together near the outer margin.

Acanthocardia tuberculata is widely distributed along the shores of European seas, the Atlantic and the Mediterranean. It occurs in large numbers on muddy, sandy and gravelly bottoms into which it burrows.

Like most other cockles, it too is popular as food and therefore widely harvested and often sold in markets. The solid ornamental shells are frequently used as ashtrays and to make other useful and ornamental objects.

Smooth Venus

Veneridae

Callista chione Linné

This species has a massive, thick, heavy shell of sloping, ovoid shape. The two valves are equal and very convex. It reaches up to 110 mm in length, 85 mm in height and 48 mm in thickness.

The surface is almost smooth with fine concentric lines that are just barely discernible. The colour is a reddish-brown often tinged with pink and with darker brown bands radiating from the beaks to the margins.

Callista chione is widespread in the littoral zone of the Mediterranean and occurs in vast numbers particularly in localities where the sand is covered with a layer of fine organic sediment. It is invisible at first glance, however, for it lives buried in the sand, extending only its long fleshy siphons above the surface. The water sucked up through the inhalent siphon provides the animal not only with oxygen for breathing but also with minute planktonic particles which it strains from the water as food. If disturbed it rapidly withdraws the siphons into the mud.

C. chione is an edible species and therefore widely gathered and sold regularly at markets.

Warty Venus

Veneridae

Venus verrucosa LINNÉ

Warty Venus is the somewhat unattractive name given to this species which has a thick, ovoid, convex shell growing to as much as 60 mm in length, 55 mm in height and 38 mm in thickness. The surface is marked by rugged sculpturing consisting of raised concentric ribs of unequal height and thickness. Towards the anterior and posterior margins these plate-like ribs are crossed by radiating ribs with wart-like processes. The beaks are only slightly raised.

The surface is comparatively drab, generally unicoloured, but may be white, yellowish or brownish-yellow. The inside of the shell is white.

Venus verrucosa is a very common and plentiful species in the littoral and sublittoral zones of the Mediterranean and Atlantic coast of south-western Europe. It occurs chiefly on sandy and muddy sediments on the seabed as well as in fine gravel, into which it burrows.

Its method of escaping from slow-moving enemies such as starfish is to make small jumps and somersaults as do other members of this genus.

It is an edible species and is gathered in many places, being sold at the markets of coastal towns as food.

Smooth Artemis

Veneridae

Dosinia lupinus LINNÉ

Dosinia lupinus has a medium-large, fairly thick shell that is round in outline. It is as long as it is high – up to 30 mm – and is 14 mm thick. The porcelain-smooth surface is sculptured with delicate concentric striations and somewhat coarser growth lines. The milky colour changes into yellow towards the beak.

This species is found on the sandy and muddy bottoms of flat, shallow shorelines from the low tide mark downward. It burrows about five centimetres deep in the sand, extending only its siphon tubes to the surface. It is very common on the European coast of the Atlantic and Mediterranean.

Rayed Artemis

Dosinia exoleta LINNÉ

Dosinia exoleta is slightly more robust than the preceding species but has a similar shape, growing to a length of 50 mm, a height of 46 mm and a thickness of 24 mm. The surface of the shell is marked with fine concentric striations and more pronounced growth lines. The white to yellowish-brown ground colour is ornamented with irregular spots.

It occurs on the European coast of the Atlantic from southern Norway to North Africa and is also found throughout the whole of the Mediterranean.

It lives in sand in similar localities to *D. lupinus*.

Dosinia lupinus 1
Dosinia exoleta 2

1
2

Striped Venus

Veneridae

Chamelea gallina LINNÉ

Chamelea gallina has a thick shell with a sloping, triangular, rounded shape. The beaks are raised and point forward. The lunule is broad and sharply demarcated. The shell grows up to 43 mm in length, 39 mm in height and 24 mm in thickness, and the valves are marked with a dense sculpture of irregular concentric ribs that are often doubled at the posterior end. The ground colour is white or pale yellow to brownish, often ornamented with three darker rays that become wider towards the margin.

This bivalve inhabits sandy and muddy bottoms, in which it burrows, at depths of four to fifty-five metres. It is very common on the Atlantic coast, its range extending as far as the North Sea. It is also found throughout the Mediterranean and in the Black Sea.

Oval Venus

Timoclea ovata PENNANT

Timoclea ovata is much smaller than the above species, growing to a length of about 15 mm, a height of 12 mm and a thickness of 7 mm. The shell is nearly triangular in shape with the beak located almost in the centre. The lunule is very narrow. The surface sculpture consists of about fifty distinct ribs radiating from the beaks to the margins. The colour may be white to pale yellow, sometimes with pale brown spots.

T. ovata is widely distributed on the European coast of the Atlantic and in the Mediterranean. It inhabits sandy bottoms at depths of twenty to sixty metres.

Chamelea gallina 1
Timoclea ovata 2

1

2

Rock-borer

Petricolidae

Petricola lithophaga RETZIUS

The layman finds it hard to accept that some species of molluscs are able to bore into fairly hard substances. One such species is *Petricola lithophaga*, which bores into limestone and sandstone. Its body structure is not as well modified for this way of life as that of the true borers – molluscs belonging to the families Pholadidae and Teredinidae (e.g. *Pholas dactylus*, the Common Piddock, or *Teredo navalis*, the Common Ship Worm).

P. lithophaga has a medium-sized, longish, ovate, flattened shell that is comparatively thin. It reaches up to 30 mm in length, 20 mm in height, and 15 mm in thickness. The surface is marked with fine sculpturing consisting of only a few concentric grooves marking the growth lines and a number of low radiating ribs and furrows. The surface is coloured greyish-white, and the inside is white.

This species occurs in large numbers on hard ground, where it bores into softer rock. Often, however, it also drills holes in the thick shells of other gastropod molluscs and sometimes even in wooden harbour constructions. It inhabits the waters of the European coast of the Atlantic, its distribution extending northward as far as the west of France and is also found in the Mediterranean and Black Sea. It causes considerable damage to harbour constructions.

The activity of borers sometimes provides interesting historical information. For example, the columns of the Temple of Serapis, built in the first century AD, are tunnelled through by borers high above the level of the temple floor. In the twelfth century, volcanic activity caused the land in the area of Naples to be covered by the sea, not to emerge again until about the sixteenth century; it was during this period that the marine borers made the tunnels in the columns.

Abrupt Wedge Shell

Donacidae

Donax trunculus Linné

The shell of *Donax trunculus* is longish and triangular. It is thin to transparent, with a rounded anterior end and a truncated posterior end. It reaches up to 40 mm in length, 24 mm in height and 11 mm in thickness. The surface is almost smooth with fine radiating striations and faint growth lines. The lower, inner edge is provided with very fine teeth along its entire length. The surface of the shell is quite drab, the ground colour being white to yellowish with irregular brownish-violet rays. The interior of the shell is usually pink in young individuals and violet in older animals.

D. trunculus is very widespread in the European seas. It inhabits the Atlantic coast from southern Norway as far as North Africa (excluding Britain) and is also found throughout the whole of the Mediterranean and Black Sea. It occurs in large numbers, mainly on muddy and sandy bottoms of the littoral zone, usually at depths of ten to fifteen metres. It burrows into the sand by extending the foot far out in front and then quickly drawing the rest of the body up to it, the animal being completely buried within four to five seconds. Food is sucked up from the sea floor through the inhalant siphon.

Despite its fairly small size this mollusc is widely gathered as food in Italy, and eaten raw.

Solecurtus strigillatus LINNÉ Psammobiidae

The shell of this species is longish, more or less rectangular in shape, and grows to a length of 80 mm, a height of 35 mm and a thickness of 20 mm. Both valves are convex and thick and rounded at both ends. The surface is plain, marked only with very fine concentric grooves crossed by twenty to twenty-five coarser, finely-waved, oblique lines. The coloration is very attractive. The whole of the outside and inside is pink with two rays, visible also on the inside, extending from the apex to the lower margin.

Solecurtus strigillatus inhabits the whole of the Mediterranean, and has also made its way to the south-western regions of the Black Sea. It is found on various types of sandy and muddy bottoms buried deep in the ground for purposes of protection, as its large fleshy body is only partly covered by the shell. All that is visible above the surface are the siphons through which water is brought to the gills, together with minute particles of food.

S. strigillatus is an edible species even though the flesh is not particularly prized. Nevertheless, it is widely gathered and sold at markets on the Mediterranean coast.

Peppery Furrow Shell

Scrobiculariidae

Scrobicularia plana DA COSTA

The shell of this bivalve is approximately ovate in shape, thin and flattened. The prominent beak is located in the centre of the shell, which reaches up to 50 mm in length, 40 mm in height and 15 mm in thickness. The surface is marked with minute concentric grooves and more pronounced growth lines. The colour is simple and drab. In older individuals the ground colour is dirty grey, in younger ones yellow-red. This coloration is due to the fact that the periostracum has not yet been worn away.

Scrobicularia plana is widely distributed from the shores of southern Norway to the coast of North Africa, also making its way into the western part of the Baltic Sea and likewise inhabiting the whole of the Mediterranean.

It is partial to the muddy and sandy bottoms of flat coasts. Most of its life is spent buried in mud, usually about fifteen centimetres deep with only the long siphon tubes protruding above the surface. With these, it probes around the area where it lies buried and, like a vacuum cleaner, sucks up matter deposited on the surface which might serve as food. It is an edible species and therefore widely gathered and often on sale at fish markets.

The shells are often washed up on flat, sandy shores in vast numbers.

Flat Tellin

Tellinidae

Angulus planatus **Linné**

This is a common, robust species of bivalve with a thin, triangular shell distinctly compressed at the sides. The beak is located more or less in the centre and the posterior end forms a sharp angle at about the midpoint. The shell reaches up to 65 mm in length, 45 mm in height and 15 mm in thickness. The surface is almost entirely smooth with fine concentric grooves. The white ground colour changes to orange-yellow towards the centre and the apex, as does the glossy porcellaneous inside wall.

Angulus planatus is widespread throughout the whole of the Mediterranean and in the Atlantic on the south-west coast of Europe. It is a common species, usually found on sandy and muddy bottoms. It also burrows into mud and sand, the flat shell penetrating the seabed with ease. The diet consists of organic sediment, microscopic seaweed and other organisms. This food is sucked up by one of the two long siphons, which move independently of each other, and is brought by the incurrent stream of water to the filtering apparatus in the gill chamber.

A. planatus is an edible species and widely gathered by offshore fishermen because of its size. It is often sold at the markets of coastal towns. The attractive shells are also used to make various fancy goods.

Thin Tellin

Tellinidae

Angulus tenuis DA COSTA

The shell of *Angulus tenuis* is of medium size, triangular to oval, flattened at the sides and thin. The posterior end has a sharp downward slant and is beak-shaped toward the rear; the anterior end is longish and oval. It reaches up to 25 mm in length, 17 mm in height and 4 mm in thickness. The surface sculpturing consists of dense concentric bands and deeper growth lines.

The delicate and fragile look is accentuated by the coloration ranging from white through yellow to rose with pale concentric bands of varying widths.

A. tenuis inhabits the European coast of the Atlantic, its distribution extending northwards as far as Norway. It occurs also in the whole of the Mediterranean and Black Sea and has even made its way to the Sea of Azov, which is an indication of its tolerance to low salinity. It frequents mainly muddy and sandy bottoms of flat shorelines. It is a deposit feeder, sucking up matter deposited on the sea floor through the inhalent siphon. Being an abundant species it plays an important role in the diet of certain commercially valuable fish that seek their food on the seabed, especially halibut.

Empty shells are washed up on the sandy shores in large numbers.

Baltic Tellin

Tellinidae

Macoma balthica LINNÉ

This species has a fairly thin shell of medium size that is rather globular with a forward-pointing raised beak. The anterior end is broadly rounded, the posterior rather pointed and beak-shaped. The length may be as much as 20 mm, the height 17 mm and the thickness 9 mm.

The glossy, porcellaneous surface is a delicate pastel hue, usually yellowish or pink, sometimes also white, frequently showing darker concentric growth lines.

Macoma balthica has a very widespread distribution. It occurs on the western coast of Europe from the Arctic Ocean to the shores of Africa and because of its tolerance of low salinities it also occurs in large numbers in the Baltic Sea. It is common throughout the Mediterranean and is also found in the brackish waters of river estuaries. In waters with a low salinity, however, it attains lesser dimensions. The best conditions for this tellin are muddy and sandy bottoms at depths of two to twenty-five metres. In suitable locations, particularly in river estuaries, it multiplies in vast numbers and it is not unusual to find as many as five thousand individuals per square metre in such places. As a rule, however, the animals live buried in the mud and not on the surface. Its mass occurrence and the thinness of its shell make *M. balthica* an important source of food for certain commercially valuable fish, chiefly halibut.

Razor Shell

Solenidae

Ensis arcuata LINNÉ

This species has a large, very long and narrow shell with blunt ends resembling a razor holder.

It reaches a length of 155 mm, a height of 18 mm and a thickness of 12 mm. The periostracum is smooth and glossy and easily peeled off dead and empty shells.

The colour is yellowish-white to greenish-brown with brown bands marking the growth lines. The interior of the shell is chalky white.

Ensis arcuata is widely distributed along the coast of Europe from Norway through the Mediterranean and on to the Black Sea. It inhabits sandy and muddy bottoms, generally buried just below the surface of the seabed with its short siphon tubes projecting. Sometimes, however, it burrows deeper, as much as one metre below the surface. This movement is effected by the foot, which can be expanded into the shape of a club; it is extended far out of the shell and then rapidly contracts, pulling the shell downwards. The process is aided by the stream of water the animal pumps from its siphon tubes.

E. arcuata is widely used as food and in many places is gathered in large numbers and sold at fish markets.

Trough Shell

Mactridae

Mactra corallina LINNÉ

This species has a rather thin shell of triangular to oval shape, growing up to 55 mm in length, 45 mm in height and 28 mm in thickness. The raised apex is blunt and nearly central.

The surface is marked with fine concentric lines, but is otherwise smooth and glossy. The coloration may be white to yellow-brown with darker concentric and sometimes also radiating bands.

Mactra corallina has a very widespread geographic distribution. In the Atlantic its range extends from the Canary Islands northward as far as southern Norway. It does not occur in the Baltic but is plentiful throughout the Mediterranean and is also found in the Black Sea.

It inhabits muddy bottoms, generally at depths of twenty to thirty metres, often descending to depths of as much as fifty-five metres. It burrows in mud and in sand, facilitating the process by ejecting a sudden stream of water from the mantle cavity, which helps break up the more compact sediment. The animal sucks microscopic food particles from the water through the siphons which it extends above the surface of the seabed.

In muddy localities it often occurs in great masses. It is an edible species that is harvested in large quantities and often sold in the fish markets. In northern Italy it is commonly eaten under the name 'biberon'. It is also an important source of food for commercially valuable fish. The firm shells are often washed up in vast numbers on sandy shores.

Common Sand Gaper

Myidae

Mya arenaria LINNÉ

The shell of *Mya arenaria* is strong, longish and ovate, rounded at the front end and slightly pointed at the rear. The left valve is generally smaller than the right one. This is a very robust species attaining a length of 120 mm, a height of 60 mm and a thickness of 40 mm. The surface is marked by coarse concentric growth lines and also by faint rays. The shell is coloured white but the periostracum is brownish.

M. arenaria is a generally distributed species, ranging from northern Europe to the Mediterranean but not the Arctic. The great adaptability and tolerance of low salinities of this bivalve is borne out by its mass occurrence in the Baltic Sea. It has also been found in the Black Sea, where it was apparently introduced.

M. arenaria lives buried as much as twenty centimetres deep in mud and sand, extending only its long, brown, connected siphon tubes to the water above. When disturbed it rapidly retracts these tubes below the surface, at the same time ejecting a stream of water.

M. arenaria is harvested in large numbers as food in many places.

Common Basket Shell

Aloididae

Corbula gibba OLIVI

This species is a typical representative of a family of small to minute asymmetrical bivalves with a world-wide distribution. The illustrated shell is triangular to oval in shape, the anterior end being round and the posterior end somewhat drawn out with one or two blunt keels. The valves are unequal; the right valve is higher and more convex with a broad, very inflated apex, its ventral edge overlapping the left valve. It grows to a length of about 16 mm, a height of 14 mm and a thickness of 8 mm. The surface sculpturing, consisting of fine concentric grooves, is also different on each valve. The coloration is quite sober, being white tinged with pink or violet-rufous. The periostracum is brown.

Corbula gibba has a widespread geographic distribution. In the eastern Atlantic its range extends from the Canary Islands as far as Norway and it is also found in the western regions of the Baltic, though there it attains much smaller dimensions (only about 8 mm in length). It is also widespread in the Mediterranean, Aegean Sea and Sea of Marmara, from where it has made its way as far as the south-western regions of the Black Sea.

It makes its home on soft muddy and sandy bottoms and is most plentiful at depths of about fifteen to thirty metres. In suitable localities it occurs in large numbers and is an important source of food for commercially valuable fish, chiefly halibut.

Flask Shell

Gastrochaenidae

Gastrochaena dubia PENNANT

The shell of this bivalve is unusual both in shape and structure. It is comparatively small, thin and fragile, the outline being an oval wedge shape. The anterior end is very short and narrow, whilst the hind end is much enlarged and elliptical. It attains a length of 20 mm, a height of 10 mm and a thickness of 8 mm. The surface is ornamented with a great number of fine, concentric lines. The shell itself is white but is often covered with a rufous-brown periostracum.

Gastrochaena dubia is a delicate and fragile mollusc. It lives solitarily in limestone, into which it bores holes, though paradoxically it also contributes to building it up. It does this by cementing pieces of limestone, minute stones and shell fragments together into a flask-shaped jacket around its shell and long siphon tubes. Frequently, however, it also bores holes into much harder matter such as the shells of various gastropods and bivalves, thereby sometimes causing great damage, e.g. in beds of oysters, where it is particularly common.

It occurs throughout the Mediterranean, and also ranges as far as the Black Sea. On the Atlantic coast its distribution extends as far as Great Britain.

Common Piddock

Pholadidae

Pholas dactylus **LINNÉ**

Pholas dactylus has a thin, elongated shell, shaped like the fruit of the date palm, beaked and narrowing to a point at the front end. It grows to a length of 150 mm, a height of 33 mm and a thickness of 35 mm. The surface is prominently sculptured with concentric and radiating ribs covered with raised, prickly teeth. The two halves of the shell are not hinged and can be moved freely against each other. The epidermis is yellowish, the shell white. *P. dactylus* is a species of boring bivalve. It drills holes in submerged peat and wood as well as in various kinds of rock, often Triassic sandstones and marls.

P. dactylus is widely distributed from Norway to the Mediterranean and on to the Black Sea. It is an edible species and in Italy is known by the name of 'dattolo di mer' (sea date).

Common Ship Worm

Teredinidae

Teredo navalis LINNÉ

For centuries *Teredo navalis* has caused immeasurable damage to the wooden parts of ships, harbour constructions, dams, bridges and other marine structures. It too is a boring bivalve, but one that lives in wood. Its gradual adaptation to this unusual way of life has caused it to look more like a worm than a mollusc. The body is very long and enclosed in a tube-like mantle. It grows to a length of more than 200 mm but is only 7–8 mm thick. The shell is reduced and occurs on the broadened front end of the body, looking like a helmet composed of two arched, three-lobed valves. A chalky tube is secreted by the mantle and this serves to line the tunnel as the Ship Worm burrows. Tunnels in wood are bored by the simultaneous action of the valves, which the animal opens and closes like pliers, and by chemical action. The fine sawdust serves as food for the animal.

Disastrous damage was caused by the Ship Worm to the merchant and war fleets of ancient times as well as to those of more recent days. The British merchant fleet suffered greatly from the ravages of this small mollusc whose penetration is very rapid. No wonder that Linné called this mollusc 'calamitas navium' (calamity of ships).

T. navalis inhabits the Atlantic, Mediterranean and Black Sea.

Thracia papyracea POLI

Thraciidae

Thracia papyracea has a thin, longish, oval shell that is somewhat asymmetrical. The two halves are unequal. The anterior end of the shell is rounded, the posterior end terminates abruptly and is narrowed. The shell reaches up to 30 mm in length, 18 mm in height and 12 mm in thickness. The surface is ornamented with fine concentric grooves and is coloured white.

T. papyracea is widespread in the Atlantic, its range extending from Iceland as far as North Africa, and it also occurs throughout the whole of the Mediterranean and Black Sea. It lives on sandy and muddy bottoms, generally at depths of between ten to fifty metres.

Crosscut Carpet Shell

Veneridae

Venerupis decussata LINNÉ

Venerupis decussata has a large shell that is ovoid when viewed from the side with the beaks uppermost. The apex is distinctly shifted towards the front. The surface is marked with a network of fine radial and concentric grooves. The ground colour is white to yellow but the whole shell is marked with a pattern of radiating irregular lines and spots.

V. decussata is widely distributed, especially in the Mediterranean. It occurs in large numbers on all types of sandy bottoms covered with organic sediment. A popular edible species, it is harvested in large quantities and sold in the markets of coastal towns, especially in winter.

Thracia papyracea 1
Venerupis decussata 2

2

Common Cuttlefish

Sepiidae

Sepia officinalis LINNÉ

In most of the existing members of the class Cephalopoda the shell is greatly reduced, enclosed by the side folds of the mantle and located on the dorsal side of the trunk.

A good example of such a shell is that of the Common Cuttlefish, *Sepia officinalis*. It is spoon-shaped with a thin horny layer on the dorsal side. Of the original shell partitions all that remains are the thin calcareous plates running obliquely from the horny layer down to the underside of the body. Shells often cast up on the sandy shores are the well known 'cuttle-bones' gathered by bird fanciers for their pets to peck at since they are a rich source of calcium. The cuttlefish grows to a length of 40–50 cm. It lives near the bottom at shallower depths and has a preference for marine growths such as seaweed. It spends most of the time, however, floating in the water, for it is an excellent swimmer. It propels itself through the water by the undulating motion of the narrow fins formed by the margin on either side; frequently, however, it makes use of the thrust produced by the rhythmical, powerful ejection of water from the mantle cavity through the pedal funnel. When in danger it uses this method to escape with rapid leaps. The cuttlefish is an edible species harvested in large numbers especially in the Mediterranean.

INDEX